Praise for
Touched by a Vampire

"Like many who care about young adults, I've puzzled over the recent vampire craze. I applaud *Touched by a Vampire* for shining its brilliant light into a somewhat dark and mysterious world. Utilizing the existing teen fascination of the Twilight books in order to spark an open discussion about love, life, and faith is both smart and savvy. This thoughtful book is a much-needed tool for parents, youth leaders, and teens."

—MELODY CARLSON, author of the Diary of a
Teenage Girl series

"'But Mom, you'd *like* this vampire book. It teaches that true love waits!' They knew which pitch to give, and Felker Jones has their number. This book is itself a page-turner, diagnosing vampiric love as meager fare. It turns out true love is not so much about waiting for Mr. Bite, but being abundantly blessed at God's banquet."

—AMY LAURA HALL, associate professor of
Christian Ethics, Duke University, and author
of *Conceiving Parenthood* and *Kierkegaard and
the Treachery of Love*

Touched
by a
Vampire

Touched
by a
Vampire

Discovering *the*
Hidden Messages
in the
Twilight Saga

BETH
FELKER JONES

MULTNOMAH
BOOKS

TOUCHED BY A VAMPIRE
PUBLISHED BY MULTNOMAH BOOKS
12265 Oracle Boulevard, Suite 200
Colorado Springs, Colorado 80921

Scripture quotations are taken from the Holy Bible, New International Version®. NIV®. Copyright © 1973, 1978, 1984 by International Bible Society. Used by permission of Zondervan Publishing House. All rights reserved.

Italics in Scripture quotations reflect the author's added emphasis.

The characters and events in this book are fictional, and any resemblance to actual persons or events is coincidental.

ISBN 978-1-60142-278-1
ISBN 978-1-60142-279-8 (electronic)

Published in the United States by WaterBrook Multnomah, an imprint of the Crown Publishing Group, a division of Random House Inc., New York

MULTNOMAH and its mountain colophon are registered trademarks of Random House Inc.

Library of Congress Cataloging-in-Publication Data
Jones, Beth Felker, 1976–
    Touched by a vampire : discovering the hidden messages in the Twilight saga / Beth Felker Jones.—1st ed.
        p. cm.
    ISBN 978-1-60142-278-1—ISBN 978-1-60142-279-8 (electronic) 1. Meyer, Stephenie, 1973– Twilight series 2. Meyer, Stephenie, 1973—Religion. 3. Bible—In literature. 4. Children's literature, American—Religious aspects. 5. Vampires in literature. I. Title.
    PS3613.E979Z73 2009
    813'.6—dc22
                                        2009028425

Printed in the United States of America
2010

10 9 8 7 6 5 4 3

For my girls

Acknowledgments
I'm grateful to students with whom I've discussed many of the questions of this book and to Ella Myer for early feedback. Many thanks to those friends who've offered support during the writing process, especially to Traci, Lynn, Tiffany, Aimee, and Dana for reading parts of the manuscript. Enormous thanks also to Jessica Barnes at WaterBrook Multnomah—truly an amazing editor! And, always, thanks to my family, to my husband, Brian, and to Gwen, Sam, and Tess. When I told Sam the book was done, he cheered.

A Note from the Author:
Resources for Using This Book

Before we start talking about the Twilight Saga and the messages it contains, I want to point out a few helpful resources you can use to start discussion about the subjects this book covers, be it in a youth group, Bible study, Sunday school class, or just a group of friends.

First of all, at the end of each chapter, you'll find questions for reflection. These questions will prompt thought about the way each chapter's theme relates to our own lives, leading to discussion about what we should take away from the Twilight Saga—and what we shouldn't.

Second, in the back of the book, there's a book-by-book discussion guide that addresses the events of each novel in the Twilight Saga and the themes and messages they portray.

In addition to these two discussion guides included in the book, there is also a leaders' guide online (www.waterbrook multnomah.com), which will give you ideas about how to use the book's discussion guide in your group.

With these resources, I hope you'll be able to discuss the topics we'll cover in this book in even more depth. This is great opportunity, not just to talk about books you love, but to draw closer to God.

Table of Contents

Introduction

I love a good story.

I love the way stories electrify my children. Some days, my son is a monster out of a storybook, threatening his sisters with terrifying growls. My daughter, maybe, acts out a fairy tale and flies through the house with sparkling wings. Or they all go outside and join the neighbors in a game of *Star Wars*. Good battles evil under the apple tree in the front yard.

I love the way a story can carry us into another world, a world of imagination and mystery. When a story captures our hearts, we dive into it. We sink deep into the waters of the world the author has created for us and learn its geography. We fear what the characters fear and love what the characters love.

Most of all, I love what happens when we come out of the story world. We come up from under the water of imagination and take a deep breath of the air of our own world. But it isn't the same world it was before we dove into the story. The story world changes our world. It helps us imagine possibilities we couldn't possibly have seen before. It suggests new dreams to guide us, new fears to horrify us, and new hopes to inspire us. The stories we love have power. They change our lives.

The power of stories led me to write this book. Maybe you've read Stephenie Meyer's Twilight Saga, and you were drawn into the story she tells. Maybe your friends have read them and told you how much they were absorbed by the world of Twilight. Maybe you're a parent and you want to know about the stories your daughter loves, or you're looking for guidance about what you want her to read.

The books are massive bestsellers. The series is popular partly because it deals with issues most of us identify with. It's about romance. It's about finding, losing, and keeping love. It's also about sex and desire. It's about family. It's even about the meaning of life. And the series is especially popular with girls and women because it's about all these things from *a girl's perspective*. There are important male characters in the books, of course, but it is through a girl's eyes, Bella's eyes, that we view the world of Twilight. It's through a girl's eyes that the story makes us think about these powerful subjects—romance, desire, sex, love, family, and meaning. I wrote this book because I'm passionate about the way these themes matter in our lives. Because I'm a Christian, because my life is shaped by the love of Jesus Christ, I especially care about how we can think about these issues through Christian eyes.

I want us to deal with the powerful themes that make the world of Twilight run, and I suggest we do so in a thoroughly Christian way. The themes of love, romance, sex, family, and meaning are central to who we are and how we live. That means we need to deal with them thoughtfully and biblically. In this book, I offer some tools and questions and ideas to help you do just that.

The themes of Twilight are all about what it means to be female. I want us to think about what it means to be female and to love God.

INTRODUCTION TO THE STORIES

Before we dig into these interesting themes, I'll give you a brief outline of the Twilight Saga. If you haven't read the books and you don't want me to ruin any surprises for you, stop right here.

Meyer's novels are fun to read. The plots take surprising twists and turns, and the four novels come together to tell a compelling love story. Bella, the heroine, is a girl-next-door teenager. She sees herself as ordinary and unremarkable. Edward is an impossibly good-looking classmate who turns out to be a vampire. In *Twilight,* they find each other and enter into unlikely love. In *New Moon,* their love seems lost. They are reunited in *Eclipse* and build a life together in *Breaking Dawn.* Along the way, they must face the dangers and darkness of the vampire world.

Twilight

Bella, whose mother wants to travel with her new husband, moves to a small, rainy town in the Pacific Northwest to live with her dad. Always one to avoid the spotlight, she isn't excited about life at her new school. A number of local boys find her very attractive, but Bella is not interested in them. Not, at least, until she becomes aware of the gorgeous and mysterious Edward. Once Edward enters her thoughts, he never leaves.

Bella sits next to Edward in science class, and his reaction is bizarre. He looks at her with hatred and utter hostility. Bella is frustrated and annoyed. What has she, an ordinary girl, done to evoke such a strong reaction in this beautiful boy?

Then Edward uses his body to stop an out-of-control van from crushing Bella in the school parking lot. He denies what Bella has started to believe—that there is something extraordinary about him. With a bit of help from her friend Jacob and the Internet, she realizes Edward is a vampire. She has discovered his deep secret, and the stage is set for the two to fall in love.

We learn that Edward is a member of a family of "vegetarian" vampires. They deny their desire for human blood and live instead by hunting large animals. Bella learns, though, that Edward's strong and horrified reaction to her when they met was because the scent of *her* blood is exceptionally tempting to him. Just sitting next to him threatened to undo his years of self-control. In the context of this danger, they begin their secret romance.

That danger increases when Bella is exposed to some ordinary murderous vampires while spending time with Edward's family. James, a vampire whose talent and sport is in tracking his prey, sets his sights on Bella, determined to hunt her down and kill her. Edward and his family craft a plan to save Bella.

They send her to Phoenix, but James lures her into a deathtrap in a mirrored dance studio.

Edward saves Bella just in time and destroys James. But Bella has suffered a bite, and Edward manages to suck the vampire venom from her blood. At the end of the novel, he refuses Bella's pleas to change her into a creature like him so she can share his life.

New Moon

At Bella's birthday party at Edward's house, Bella accidentally gets cut, and the scent of her blood topples the shaky self-control of Edward's brother Jasper. He rushes to attack her and has to be stopped by his family. This incident shakes Edward to the core. Convinced that he cannot love Bella and keep her safe, he leaves her.

Bella sinks into a dark depression. Much of the novel is about the depths of her sadness and brokenness in the face of lost love.

Eventually, Bella finds some comfort in her growing friendship with Jacob. She and Jacob fix up a pair of old motorcycles, an activity her father has forbidden because he has seen so many motorcycle accidents. The thrill of riding the motorcycle causes Bella to hear Edward's voice in her head, which motivates her to try more dangerous activities in an effort to be closer to him.

Strange happenings in Jacob's community lead to the eventual disclosure that he has become a werewolf. In the world of Twilight, these werewolves exist for one specific purpose—to protect human life from vampires. As a werewolf, Jacob protects Bella from the vampire Victoria, who seeks revenge against Bella for the death of James in *Twilight*.

In another dangerous moment, Bella tries cliff diving and nearly drowns. Though Jacob rescues her from the ocean, Edward is misinformed. Believing Bella is dead, Edward goes to Italy to commit suicide by provoking the Volturi, the leaders of the vampire realm.

Bella and Edward's sister Alice set off in a dramatic race to get to Italy in time to save Edward. Though they succeed, the Volturi learn of Bella's relationship with Edward and pose a new threat to her safety. Because she knows about them, they decree that she must either be killed or become a vampire herself. Becoming a vampire is exactly what Bella wants, but Edward continues to refuse her.

Bella realizes that Edward left her in order to protect her. Their relationship is cemented more tightly than ever before.

Eclipse

Bella agrees to trade something she doesn't want to do—getting married—for something Edward doesn't want to do—turning her into a vampire.

Edward and his family suspect that a number of murders

in Seattle are being caused by uncontrolled vampire activity. Victoria's threat to Bella still looms, as does the question of whether and when Bella will become a vampire. Suspense builds on both counts. In addition, Bella has to negotiate her love for Edward in light of the loving friendship that grew between her and Jacob while Edward was gone.

The threat in Seattle is uncovered. Victoria is creating an army of vampires to destroy Bella, Edward, and his family. We learn that "newborn" vampires, those who have only recently been turned, are especially strong and vicious.

Though they are natural enemies, Edward's vampire family and Jacob's werewolf pack form an unlikely alliance to defeat Victoria and her army. Bella is forced to deal with the tensions in her relationships with Edward and Jacob. She realizes her love for Jacob, but she chooses Edward. At the end of the novel, Jacob, unable to deal with his sadness over losing Bella, runs away.

Breaking Dawn

Bella and Edward have a beautiful wedding at his family's home, and they travel to an island paradise for their honeymoon. The trip is cut short when Bella discovers she is pregnant and that the baby seems to be growing at an alarming rate. Edward, concerned for her safety, wants her to end her pregnancy, but Bella, haunted by dreams in which a beautiful child who looks like Edward is in danger, is determined to protect the baby at any cost.

For the next section of the novel, the pregnancy makes Bella incredibly weak. As though she doesn't have the strength to continue her story on her own, the narrative shifts into Jacob's voice. Jacob and Edward are united in their horror at what the vampire baby is doing to Bella. When it seems she will die, they manage to buy her time by getting her human blood to drink. At the moment of her death—the baby's violent birth—Edward finally changes Bella into a vampire.

After her painful transformation, Bella makes tentative steps into her new life. Her new vampire family is intent on protecting her from taking human life during her vicious, bloodthirsty newborn phase. Bella, though, surprises everyone with her self-control and her vampire skill. She is able to enjoy her relationship with Edward and their daughter, Renesmee. She even finds some peace in her friendship with Jacob.

The Volturi believe that little Renesmee is an illegal "immortal child." Vampires are prohibited from turning human children into vampires, because the little ones never learn to control themselves and threaten the secrecy and stability of the vampire world. Like the other books, *Breaking Dawn* culminates with a threat and a showdown as the Volturi threaten to destroy Edward, Bella, and their family.

The family gathers friends around them in an attempt to make the Volturi pause long enough to listen to the truth. Bella trains for a fight and practices a "shield" power that helps protect her family. The Cullens manage to convince the Volturi that

Renesmee is not a threat to their society, and the series ends with the family able to look forward to peace and happiness together.

USING THIS BOOK

Now that you're familiar with the story, this book will be your guide through some of the most pressing themes of the Twilight Saga.

I've heard many suggestions that Christians should embrace Meyer's series. Because the universe she writes about is a moral universe, maybe Christians can find our own morality there. Because her couple waits until marriage to have sex, maybe Christians can draw an encouraging word about purity and self-control.

I'm hesitant about these suggestions.

I think Christians can draw plenty of goodness from non-Christian stories, but I'm doubtful about the way themes of morality and goodness work in the Twilight Saga. Meyer is Mormon, and her books paint a deeply Mormon picture of the universe. The books also reflect the values and assumptions of American popular culture in some ways that we as Christians will want to notice. I'm here to help you ask questions, to help you look at the themes of the Twilight universe from a Christian point of view.

As I said, Meyer's stories are fun to read, but not everything that compels us is healthy. I hope you'll use this book for discernment. I hope you'll learn to see what builds you up and what tears you down. As Christians, we need to develop skills that will help us to see what is healthy and what is not. Some stories will nourish us, will help us to grow strong in faith, and will encourage us to know and love Jesus better. Other stories may be less like a balanced meal and more like a can of soda and a candy bar. Junk food won't hurt us once in a while, but it won't help us grow strong either. Still other stories may function more like poison. They may turn our hearts away from loving God and toward other kinds of desire.

I'm not here to tell you what stories you should or shouldn't read. I'm not going to prescribe a list of books that are wholesome versus those that are candy. But I would like to give you some skills that will help you stock the fridge for your own life of reading and imagination.

I'm also not here to give you *the* final interpretation of the Twilight Saga. Reading the stories, you may notice very different things than I noticed. You may not agree with my reactions to the characters or the plots. I am here to raise questions that occurred to me while I read, to point out the way things seem to work in the Saga, and to give some insight into how the themes of the Saga relate to the Christian life. I hope my questions will help you ask questions too.

The chapters in this book are organized around the themes of the series, which I mentioned earlier. In each chapter, I'll talk about the way a theme operates in the Twilight story, and I'll give some suggestions for addressing the theme thoughtfully and biblically.

I hope you'll use this book for personal reflection. Maybe you have a group of Christian friends who can help you reflect on the powerful themes we're going to discuss. Maybe you can read it with a youth leader or with a group of Christians who meet together for discipleship and accountability. I'd love it if moms and daughters read this book together.

I know you care about the themes that drive the Twilight Saga. They're compelling and affect all our lives on a daily basis. Whoever you read this book with, I hope you'll discuss these themes with other Christians. They're too important to deal with alone.

Chapter 1

>→>⤙←

Forbidden Fruit

The Allure of Dangerous Romance

SUPPOSE THAT EACH PERSON POSSESSES A certain amount of energy for wanting and hoping and wishing. This energy represents our deep longings. If we picture that energy as a pile of golden coins, we can imagine the ways we "spend" it. For many girls and women, we pour most of these coins out on romance. We spend the coins on imagining a true love, on hoping that we will meet Mr. Right, our Prince Charming. We sigh over "the one," our soul mate, the romantic love who will finally understand us, who will match up with who we are.

When we're little girls, we watch Snow White sing, "Someday my prince will come," longing for the day when she will meet the man of her dreams. According to the song, when she meets Prince Charming, it will be love at first sight. Snow White and her cousins, the princesses of all our favorite fairy tales, gladly spend their golden coins on yearning for that prince. We've been encouraged to share this longing, to make it our own story.

Bella's romance in the Twilight Saga fits with our tendency to spend our wanting and hoping coins on romance. This romance defies the rules and rushes forward despite all dangers. It is also completely absorbing—it demands everything from Bella (and from many readers of the books as well). Most of all, this romance is fated. Edward and Bella are soul mates, meant for each other. The forces that draw them together are more powerful than the difficulties and dangers that would keep them apart.

Intense and dangerous romance defines the Twilight Saga.

DANGEROUS ROMANCE

When Bella first sits down next to Edward in science class, he tenses up and looks at her with revulsion. She had noticed him earlier that day but doesn't yet know him. Bella can't imagine why she has provoked such horror from the boy next to her. His strong reaction makes her think about the phrase "If looks could kill."[1] She senses the danger between them.

We later learn why Edward looked at her with such disgust. For him, the lure of Bella's flesh, the particular scent of

---

1. Stephenie Meyer, *Twilight* (New York: Little, Brown and Company, 2005), 24.

her blood, is uniquely tempting. It is so tantalizing that he has to run away to keep himself from attacking her and undoing all the years he has spent protecting human life. Even though he has practiced restraint for decades, developing self-control, he must flee. For him, Bella is that enticing. Running is the only way to stop himself from ripping her to pieces then and there.

In *New Moon,* Aro, one of the Volturi guardians of the vampire world, is baffled at the way Edward can resist the "call" of Bella's blood when it speaks to him with such intensity. Why would Edward *want* to resist such a tempting lure? Why, when something is *that* desirable, *that* delicious, would Edward steel himself against the urge to bite?

At the beginning of *Twilight,* we meet a quotation from Scripture. In Genesis 2:17, God instructs human beings that they "must not eat from the tree of the knowledge of good and evil, for when you eat of it you will surely die." The book's striking cover art, a ripe red apple, is the forbidden fruit of dangerous love. The romance at the center of *Twilight* is forbidden because it is so very dangerous.

As Christians, though, we need to pause before we romanticize the knowledge of good and evil. In Genesis, God gives the people many, many good things. They have all they need for joy and happiness and a great life. The choice humans make to disobey God and eat the one "forbidden" fruit is, literally, a fatal choice. It brings sin and death into the world. All of that happiness and goodness come crashing down around them.

Romance threatens to destroy Bella. The books create a constant, suspenseful awareness that Edward is always in danger of losing control and biting her. Every moment that Bella and Edward are together, he struggles with his desire to drink her blood. Bella's friend Mike expresses his distaste for her growing relationship with Edward. "He looks at you," Mike says, "like...like you're something to eat."[2]

Before spending time alone with each other, Edward prepares carefully, taking precautions to keep Bella safe. He makes sure that he isn't overly hungry. He does all he can to fight against the temptation of her very presence, especially if they leave the watchful eyes of others. He must prepare because his nature is, for Bella, life-threatening. Bella, though, seems unconcerned about her own danger. Instead, she worries that it would cause trouble for Edward if she were murdered on his watch.

Bella does admit, at least at moments, to finding Edward frightening. When he drops his "carefully cultivated façade"[3] of humanity, he is both frightening and beautiful to Bella. Her attraction to him is tied up with the fact that he is dangerous.

Repeatedly, Bella confuses Edward by embracing the danger that lies in being with him. He tries, again and again, to warn her off for her own good. She refuses, again and again, to remove herself from this perilous situation.

---

2. *Twilight*, 221.
3. *Twilight*, 264.

Romance in the series is something dangerous and illicit. That is, it is against the law. Every rule of both human and vampire society is working against the couple. He threatens her existence with his thirst for her blood. She threatens his existence when she discovers his secret life. Bella and Edward want what they simply shouldn't have.

So how should Christians view illicit romance?

To start with, we don't exist alone. God has created us to live in community, and we do that as the church. The church exists as both the body and the bride of Jesus. Christians, then, are never rogue agents. We're parts of a body. Paul, in 1 Corinthians, puts it like this:

The eye cannot say to the hand, "I don't need you!"
And the head cannot say to the feet, "I don't need
you!" (12:21)

We need each other. We need each other in the area of romance just as in every other area of life. Other members of the body can help us to see things that we couldn't have seen on our own. They can help us discern whether our romantic interests are really in our *best* interests. They can help us to discern whether our romantic interests are in *God's* interests. Parents, pastors, Christian friends, and youth leaders can *be* the church for us in helping us to think about romance.

This idea that the church should have a role in our romantic stories is a grating one. I understand if you'd rather head for a long, painful visit to the dentist than ask for someone else's opinion about who you should or shouldn't dream about.

The idea of romantic accountability irritates us because we think of romance as a very private thing. Bella and Edward certainly do. Bella hides the truth about Edward from her parents. She ignores Jacob's feelings about the dangers of her relationship. Though Edward's family eventually grows to love Bella, he deliberately ignores their early worries about the complications involved with him loving a human girl. He breaks the vampire taboo against revealing his world to a human. Their attraction to one another is so very strong that it seems there is nothing for them to do but ignore the rules meant to keep them safe.

Yet nothing in the Christian life is truly private. We belong, after all, to God and not to ourselves. While this idea seems to go against the way we want romance to be, it is actually one of God's very good gifts. God made us so that we shouldn't be alone, and God didn't do this to annoy us. God doesn't give us the church to impose a bunch of arbitrary rules on us. God gives us the church as a blessing. The fact that you are not alone is a good thing. It means you're not at your own mercy.

You and I both know that the church is not a perfect place. It is a place for sinners, so we can't expect the church's efforts to help us be discerning about romance to be perfect either.

It helps, though, to remember that the church exists for a reason. It exists for God's glory. It exists to be Jesus's holy bride.

When we ask the church—parents, friends, leaders—to hold us accountable about romance, we're not giving people license to control us with whatever their own preferences might happen to be. We're not asking, for instance, if someone else thinks this or that person is physically attractive. I can imagine all kinds of really bad reasons why people might think we shouldn't be attracted to someone. If someone dislikes a person because of his race or because he isn't from a wealthy family, we as Christians wouldn't find any help for accountability there. Still, we *need* accountability. We're asking other people to help us *be* the church, to glorify God and become His holy bride, in every area of life. Including romance.

As we look for accountability in the area of romance, we have a way to tell what good romance or bad romance is like. If attraction to someone else glorifies God, this is a good sign. If the person who captures our romantic interest is good at serving Jesus and helps us be good at it, this too is a good sign. When we're caught up in romantic feelings, these good signs may be the kind of thing we miss. Worse, we may miss bad signs, like our attraction to someone pulling us away from God or encouraging us to be less than the people God wants us to be. We may even miss it if our attraction is actually putting us in danger.

Step outside of Bella's shoes for a moment, and imagine you were her best friend. Would you have been worried about the danger involved in her romance with Edward? Romance should not be dangerous. We have jokes and stereotypes about girls being attracted to "bad boys," but the truth is that those attractions often cause a lot of pain. Bella's disregard for her own safety is a warning sign, one we should pay attention to if we see it in ourselves or our friends. We especially need account-ability when we might be putting ourselves in danger.

CONSUMING ROMANCE

The romance in Twilight is all-consuming. When she falls in love with Edward, Bella doesn't have space for anything else in her life. The books use words like *obsessed* or *consumed* to describe Bella's feelings for Edward. Edward influences everything Bella thinks and does. She is willing to surrender her entire life for Edward, ready, in his words, "for this to be the twilight" of life, "…ready to give up everything."[4] Readers of Twilight are consumed by this romance too. I've heard plenty of accounts of the series eating up all of someone's time and energy, almost swallowing her up.

As Christians, we have to be immediately suspicious of an account of romance that consumes our entire being. One of the strongest warnings in Scripture is against idolatry. Again and again, the people turn away from God's commandments:

---

4. *Twilight*, 497.

You shall have no other gods before me. You shall
not make for yourself an idol in the form of anything in heaven above or on the earth beneath or in
the waters below. You shall not bow down to them
or worship them; for I, the LORD your God, am a
jealous God. (Exodus 20:3–5)

In the New Testament, Paul describes the sad state of living in idolatry. We human beings have become fools and "ex-
changed the glory of the immortal God for images made to
look like mortal man and birds and animals and reptiles"
(Romans 1:23). We've made a bad trade, Paul is saying. We've
traded in God's glory for sad images. While you and I probably don't pray to an idol carved to look like a bird or a rep-
tile, we are still tempted to idolatry. We're tempted to trade
the most amazing, priceless, astounding thing in the world—
the glory of the immortal God—for images. We trade God's
glory for illusions.

Is there anything that demands you give allegiance to it before you give glory to God? That thing is an idol. Is there anything that wants to consume your whole life, to take from you
all your energy and longing and wishing and hoping? That
thing is an idol. It is easy for romance to become such an idol.

Paul continues his description of idolatry in the first chapter of Romans. Not only do human beings make this bad trade,
but the trade has consequences. What happens to human beings

when we trade in God's glory for something else? We're handed over to our sinful desires. We're trapped.

The message of the Bible is that God should be the center of our lives. Jesus highlights this message when He quotes from the book of Deuteronomy:

> Love the Lord your God with all your heart and
> with all your soul and with all your mind and with
> all your strength. (Mark 12:30)

Jesus is not talking about loving God halfway. He's not talking about spending half of your energy on God and half on other things. Jesus repeats the word *all* four times in the verse above. How should we love God? With all that we are. With heart, soul, mind, and strength. With passion, longing, thought, and energy. With desire, time, attention, and activity. In Jesus, we see someone whose whole life is about God. He offers us the chance to have the same kind of life.

FATED ROMANCE

More than anything else, romance in the Twilight universe is something fated. Bella and Edward are meant for each other. They are the ideal of what romantic soul mates should be. Their connection is powerful, immediate, and irresistible. They are drawn to each other, pulled together as though by a magnetic force. Bella seems to exist just for Edward. Her very makeup, who she is at the core, is a perfect match for his desire.

In addition to Bella and Edward's romance, the series portrays another strong instance of fated romance. In Jacob's werewolf pack, werewolves find romance through "imprinting." When he meets the "one," the fated love, the werewolf immediately imprints on the other person. Jacob describes this in strong terms. He explains to Bella, "It's not like love at first sight, really. It's more like…gravity moves. When you see her, suddenly it's not the earth holding you here anymore. She does. And nothing matters more than her."[5] Imprinted pairs experience "peace and certainty."[6]

Sam, the leader of Jacob's pack, has imprinted on a woman named Emily. Sam accidentally harmed Emily when he was in his wolf phase. Before he imprinted on Emily, though, Sam was in a committed relationship with someone else, Leah, but when he imprints, he has no choice but to leave Leah behind. The treatment of Leah's situation in the series is incredibly frustrating. Her rage and pain at Sam's rejection isn't handled with much seriousness. Sam, in the romantic world of Meyer's series, has no control over this rejection. The bonds of a loving relationship cannot hold him when fate steps in and he imprints on Emily.

---

5. Stephenie Meyer, *Eclipse* (New York: Little, Brown and Company, 2007), 176.
6. Stephenie Meyer, *Breaking Dawn* (New York: Little, Brown and Company, 2008), 153.

Emily also receives very little attention in the narrative. We see that the injury Sam caused her is a source of pain, particularly for him, but we don't see much about the difficulty of living with and loving a werewolf who unintentionally scarred you. We don't hear much of Emily's voice or about what choice she had in loving Sam. She would, presumably, have had very little choice if fate truly meant her to be with him.

We hear even less of the voices of other characters imprinted on by werewolves. Jacob's friend Quil imprints on a child named Claire. The reader is assured that there is nothing inappropriate in his loving devotion to the toddler. Quil will not desire her romantically until she is a grown woman. For now, he is a devoted baby-sitter. But the narrative doesn't address the question of the inherent imbalance of power in a relationship between a girl and a man years older than her. Even if Quil would still be physically young when Claire grew old enough for him, he'd still have years of experience she wouldn't. It would be difficult for there to be much that was mutual about such a relationship. Quil would always have the upper hand, the stronger voice.

The assumption that romance is fated is very widespread, and it's portrayed in a compelling way in Twilight. What are the consequences of accepting this idea of romance? First, if romance is determined by fate, if my love has to be my soul mate, the one I am meant for, then the possibilities of choice and accountability disappear. I'm no longer free to make good choices about who I want to share my life with. Instead, I am bound by fate. Also, I can no longer seek the good advice of other Christians about my romantic life. Fate is the only advisor I need.

Fated romance thus not only destroys our freedom to choose at the beginning of a relationship, but it also threatens our freedom to *continue* to choose love in the face of difficulties and distractions. If I were bound by the idea of the fated romantic soul mate, I would follow him whenever I found him, even if that meant leaving someone else behind, like Sam leaves Leah for Emily. The idea of fated romance destroys good marriages in just this way. If I become convinced that someone other than my husband is actually my soul mate, then I lose the freedom God gives me to keep on loving my husband through thick and thin. I lose the freedom to continue to choose love daily, to keep my commitments, and to enjoy all the rich blessings of a steadfast love.

The idea that you belong with a soul mate, then, robs you of your freedom. It steals from you the power God gives you, through the Holy Spirit, to make good choices, choices that are for God's glory. The idea of a soul mate binds us. It wraps us in chains.

Why, then, are we so captivated by this idea? I think it's because we want to be loved by someone who is just for us, someone who really fits with who we are. We want it desperately. We're hurt and we're broken, and we want someone to meet us exactly where we are.

No human being, however, can fulfill us. No human being can complete us. No human being can give our lives meaning. If what we hope for from romance is fulfillment, completion, and meaning, we are going to be sadly disappointed. We'll demand something from another person that he or she cannot possibly give.

The good news is that we don't have to give up our hopes. But we do need to put them in the right place. God is so much more than human beings can ever be. This doesn't mean that God will do whatever you want or that you can mold God to be the way you'd like Him to be. It does mean, though, that God has a really beautiful way of meeting us exactly where we are.

God knows exactly what human need is and knows exactly what to do about it. God jumped right into the world with us. God became "flesh and made his dwelling among us" (John 1:14). God-in-the-flesh fits what we need so perfectly. Jesus is God there for us, experiencing what we experience, struggling with our struggles. He's been tempted. He's known need.

We needed to touch and see God's love for us, and God came to us as the touchable, seeable, Jesus. We needed to be healed, and Jesus took on all of our mess, all of our guilt, to heal us. We needed to know who God was, and Jesus came so that we could see "his glory" (verse 14).

This is more compelling than a consuming romance. This reaches right into the depths of our being to touch us as we truly are.

✝ THINK ABOUT IT/TALK ABOUT IT

1. What are your favorite romance stories? What makes them so compelling?

2. Who can you turn to for accountability? Wait. Don't skip over this question. I hope, if you're young, that the answer might include your parents, but if there are reasons it can't right now, do some brainstorming. A family friend? Someone at church? at school? down the block?

3. Who can you offer accountability to? Who can you help to see what kind of choices will serve God's glory?

4. Even with no vampires around, how can romance become dangerous in our lives?

5. What would it look like for romance to be about glorifying God?

6. Talk about the concept of the soul mate. Do you think it is a problematic concept? Does it have a lot of power in your life?

Chapter 2

→>—<←

Dazzled

How Love Works in the Twilight Saga

WE'VE TALKED ABOUT ROMANCE and seen the way that romantic attraction in Twilight is governed by a sense that people have little control over that attraction. When you meet your soul mate, you can't resist. So when two people have been drawn together in this way, what does the love between them look like?

For Bella and Edward, love is all-absorbing. Bella centers her entire life, her whole being, on Edward. Everything else becomes unimportant in the light of her love. Because this love is so total, so overwhelming, it is also something that can destroy. Because Bella's whole life is about Edward, love makes her exceptionally vulnerable. Without him, her very existence is threatened. She'll do anything for him. This captivating, potentially destructive love exists in uneasy tension with other kinds of love.

We'll examine the way all of this operates in the world of Twilight. What does it look like? How does it compare to the love God promises?

SATELLITE LOVE

Love takes over Bella's and Edward's lives because they complete one another. Each is the reason for the other's existence.

Edward spent decades believing he "was complete,"[1] but falling in love with Bella teaches him otherwise. Though his vampire "parents" and "siblings" are paired off in loving relationships, Edward believed he didn't need someone else in his life. All those years, he thought he was okay. Yet, as Meyer writes it, for all those years, his life was not whole. Then Bella changed his world. Bella gave his life the purpose he hadn't known he lacked.

Bella compares her existence without Edward to a "lost moon," a moon without a planet, circling "around the empty space left behind."[2] This is a powerful illustration for the way Edward becomes the true center of her life. She orbits around him.

---

1. Stephenie Meyer, *Twilight* (New York: Little, Brown and Company, 2005), 304.
2. Stephenie Meyer, *New Moon* (New York: Little, Brown and Company, 2006), 201.

Bella's mom, Renee, uses a similar image when she expresses concern about the intensity of her daughter's relationship with Edward. "You orient yourself around him without even thinking about it," Renee says. "When he moves, even a little bit, you adjust your position at the same time. Like magnets...or gravity. You're like a...satellite, or something."[3]

Renee worries that Bella has surrendered everything to Edward. Her every movement and thought is a response to Edward. All her choices begin with him. The way Renee sizes up the situation, Edward is the dynamic one in the relationship. He is the actor, Bella the reactor. Bella has become a *satellite*. Jacob compares Edward's effect on Bella to that of an eclipse. As an eclipse blocks the sun, preventing light from reaching the ground, Edward blocks off any possibilities for Bella but that she will be with him, belong with him, and center her life on him.

As Bella describes her love for Edward, we see that she would do anything for him. She believes she would respond to his voice under any circumstance. She would answer his call even if she were dead. The words and images she uses for her love reflect burning intensity and deep devotion. Her life is absorbed in his. To her, he is an angel, a miracle. Bella thinks Edward is perfect.

So she is angry and resentful at any suggestion that her reasons for loving Edward or her way of loving him might be

---

3. Stephenie Meyer, *Eclipse* (New York: Little, Brown and Company, 2007), 68.

questioned. She doesn't want her parents' interference. She dismisses Renee's concern that she has become a satellite, something peripheral that circles around the thing that *really* matters. Neither will she accept Jacob's warnings. Jacob's depiction of Edward as an eclipse, blocking Bella's sun, is not a picture she can or wants to challenge. Her ability to see anything but Edward has already gone. The love in the novels is the love of two people centered on one another. For both Bella and Edward, the other becomes the center of their being.

If love is about becoming a satellite, that love expects another human being to be *worth* orbiting around. Christians need to raise questions about a picture of love that assumes another human being can complete us, can be the rightful center of our world. If we think that another person can give us everything we need, if we think another person can give meaning or purpose to our lives, we are setting ourselves up to be disillusioned. We're setting ourselves up to go running off to find a new "center" the moment our human center disappoints us. No human being can possibly fulfill us.

All people are weak and limited. Our loves are not immortal, superstrong vampires. They are ordinary human beings who have annoying habits and make mistakes. The great thing is that we too are weak, limited, annoying human beings. If we think love has to be about loving someone worthy, who can complete us, we will find, first, that no other person can fill this role.

We'll also find that *we* cannot fulfill this role either. I'd be horrified if my husband tried to center his life on me. I'm terribly flawed; he'd be terribly let down. But I'm delighted that we can love each other *as* weak, limited human beings. Though I am flawed and annoying, he loves me. Though he is flawed and annoying, I love him. There is real beauty in that. We cannot be the center of each other's lives. We can, though, love each other steadily in the midst of our imperfections. But we can only do this because God is the center of our lives.

FRIENDSHIP AND LOVE

We can't discuss love in the Twilight series without paying attention to the love triangle that forms between Edward, Bella, and Jacob. For most Twilight fans, Edward has become the symbol of everything a girl could want. He is the handsome, intense love that so many long for. A smaller but vocal contingent of fans, though, prefers to focus energies on Jacob. When the novels weren't completed and it seemed possible that Bella might choose Jacob, these fans rooted for him. They lament Bella's choice of Edward over Jacob.

However else love works in the world, one fact remains: Love is complicated. We catch a glimpse at some of the ways love can be complicated as Meyer's story grows. When Edward leaves Bella in his attempt to protect her from the dangers of the vampire world, her only solace comes from her friendship with

Jacob. Jacob is a family friend, and he comes to be a best friend to Bella. He is there for her through the depression and pain that overtake her when she loses Edward. They spend long, happy hours together working on bikes and talking companionably. Though Jacob is a werewolf, he is also the boy next door, the parallel to Bella's own everygirl character. He is handsome but awkward. A leader but hesitant to lead. He loves Bella. If Edward is a drug for Bella, Jacob says, Jacob is something entirely different in her life. He tells her that their fit together is natural, that he would have been for her not heroin, but fresh air and sunshine.

Though it happens only after a lot of denial, Bella eventually recognizes some of the complications of love. She realizes that she loves both Jacob and Edward. She hates that loving both of them hurts both of them, especially Jacob. This leads Bella to deep self-loathing. Because she thinks love is supposed to be an all-consuming, irresistible force, she sees her love for *both* Edward and Jacob as deviant. She beats herself up emotionally for being untrue.

But what if feeling love for two people is not deviant, but normal? If we are freed from the ideology of the soul mate, we can view Bella's situation, caught between Jacob and Edward, quite differently than she does when she is berating herself. If love is about fated soul mates, Bella is right. Her love for both Edward and Jacob is a terrible thing. But if love is about good, healthy choices to remain committed to another human being, we can think more clearly about finding a Jacob attractive when we're already committed to an Edward. It's normal to be attracted to attractive people. It doesn't mean we were wrong all along about who our soul mates were. If we're committed to someone though, we can recognize that attraction for what it is—an acknowledgment that this other person is good, is beautiful. We can recognize it without being compelled to act on it. We can stay faithful to the one we're committed to, move past our romantic desire for the other person, and find paths to real friendship.

Love Can Destroy

Bella gives up her entire life—her relationships with parents and friends and even her humanity—in order to be with Edward. Her transformation from human to vampire is excruciatingly painful, but she hides the pain and lies about it to her love. "When you loved the one who was killing you," she says, "it left you with no options. How could you run, how could you fight, when doing so would hurt that beloved one? If your life was all you had to give your beloved, how could you not give it? If it was someone you truly loved?"[4]

When a human love becomes the center of all that you are, that love acquires the power to destroy. Bella learns that love

---

4. Stephenie Meyer, *Breaking Dawn* (New York: Little, Brown and Company, 2008), 1.

can "break you."[5] Early in the story, Edward sees the danger involved for Bella in loving him. He knows he is a threat to her, and he even admits to a certain amount of selfishness. Though he endangers her, he wants to be with Bella too much to leave her alone. He describes himself as a monster, as inhuman. He is surprised that Bella wants him anyway.

Both Bella and Edward are willing to die for each other. Bella acknowledges this early in their relationship, when she stands unwaveringly in her decision that she wants to be with Edward despite his constant thirst for her blood. The threat that their love will be the death of her is expressed in comparing him to a lion and her to a lamb.

Meyer writes about Bella and Edward operating like drugs for each other. Bella is Edward's "brand of heroin."[6] Jacob also compares Edward's role in Bella's life to that of a drug. Desire for the one you love is compared to a desire for substances that hook people, causing them to react viscerally, to want nothing else in life but to possess and to consume. The metaphor—love as a drug, love as a personal heroin—is a dark one. What does heroin do? It enslaves people. It becomes an obsession, a compulsion. Addicts leave behind family and friends, jobs and school and things that used to give them happiness, in order to get and use the drug. For many, heroin eventually kills.

Edward becomes so horrified by the danger he poses to

---

5. *New Moon*, 219.
6. *Twilight*, 267.

Bella that, in *New Moon,* he leaves her. He is trying to protect her but merely exposes her to new ways that an all-consuming love can destroy. When Edward leaves, the pain nearly annihilates Bella. She slips into a dark depression. The healthy aspects of normal life—food, friends, family, fun—hold no interest for her at all when Edward leaves. She stops taking care of herself. She becomes reckless and repeatedly flirts with death.

In *New Moon,* in which Edward and Bella spend large parts of the book apart, Edward shows that he, too, would choose to die rather than live without Bella. When he believes she is dead, he sets off for Italy to commit suicide by provoking the Volturi. He does this immediately, without pausing over the grief it will bring to his family. It isn't easy for a vampire to kill himself, but Edward's strong reaction at the thought of Bella's death sends him seeking his own death without a second thought. He will break the rules of his vampire world, threaten the secret of its existence, in order to get the Volturi to destroy him.

Because their love consumes them, it leaves Bella and Edward vulnerable, open to destruction. They risk death for each other. Bella gives up everything, including her humanity. When Edward speculates about what becoming a vampire might do to her relationship with God, she offers that to him as well. "I don't want it without you," she says of her soul, "it's yours already!"[7] Bella is ready to give Edward her entire being—body, soul, and

---

7. *New Moon,* 69.

spirit. She'll risk eternal separation from God for the sake of her love.

We shouldn't view the destructive power of the love between Bella and Edward through rose-tinted glasses. At first glance, it seems passionate and intense to think about loving someone so much that you would die for him or die without him. Death should not be taken so lightly. Death is a terrible enemy, a monster that leaves grief in its wake. Think of the effects it would have had on his family had Edward been successful in his suicide attempt.

To center our life on another human being is not just to *risk* having that center pulled away, as Bella's is when Edward leaves her. To center our life on another human being *guarantees* that center will be pulled away. No human being can or should be all that Bella and Edward demand of one another.

LOVE THAT ISN'T LOVE

Real love may be complicated, but there are ways of "loving" that aren't love at all. When love abuses, when love hurts the one who is supposed to be cared for, then love *isn't* love. Too many features of Bella's love for Edward parallel the relationships of the many real girls and women who experience abuse.

Abuse in dating and marriage relationships is an enormous problem. We can't afford to nourish any attitudes that might make abuse seem normal or acceptable. Often, what begins with one incident of abuse—a slap, a bruise—escalates until the relationship ends with an abusive husband or boyfriend killing the one he is supposed to "love." Let's take a look at some key signs of abusive relationships:

- possessiveness and jealousy
- trying to control the partner's behavior
- becoming isolated from friends or family
- the man tends to be violent, to lose his temper
- constantly checking up on the partner, always wanting to keep an eye on her
- threatening to commit suicide if the partner leaves the relationship

If we examine the list above, it is easy to see how idealizing the love between Bella and Edward might become an excuse for abuse. Edward doesn't hit Bella, but their relationship exhibits most, if not all, of these features of an abusive relationship. Edward, for instance, tries to control Bella's comings and goings. He takes parts out of her car to keep her from going to visit Jacob, and he even watches her in her sleep. His reason, of course, is that he is trying to protect her from danger, but this doesn't make him any less controlling.

If we idealize Bella and Edward's love, it may be an easy step to seeing controlling, possessive behavior as *loving* behavior. But, truly, it is anything but. Being controlling and jealous is *not* a sign of a great love. It is a sign of something dark and dangerous.

When I think about the parallels between violent and abusive relationships and love as it is depicted in Twilight, I worry about Bella's behavior and the things Bella says to herself about love even more than I worry about Edward's desire to control her.

The Twilight Saga suggests that the love between Bella and Edward is true love. If Bella and Edward are used as a measuring stick for love in real life, we may come to believe that true love looks a lot like controlling, abusive love. We may be in danger of ignoring the goodness of gentle love, love that grants freedom to the loved one, love that enjoys everyday life.

Instead of a true love, we see that Bella wants to *belong* to Edward, whatever the cost. She is willing to rationalize all kinds of dangers and threats as part of what it means to love him. The whole scope of the books is about her desire to die for him, and eventually she does.

Other members of the Cullen family are willing to change Bella from a human to a vampire, but she wants it to be Edward. Consider her thoughts on the matter: "I liked the idea that his lips would be the last good thing I would feel…I wanted his venom to poison my system. It would make me belong to him in a tangible, quantifiable way."[8] I don't know how we can read this as anything but eerie. She wants him to destroy her. When he finally changes her into a vampire, she hides her agony and suffering. She wants to take the pain with a composed face so that Edward won't know how much he has hurt her.

---

8. *Eclipse*, 324.

Dating violence and abuse is very, very common among adolescents. Teenagers can be especially vulnerable to abusive relationships because they don't have many years of experience with dating relationships and don't know if what's going on is normal or not. Teenagers are also made vulnerable by peer pressure to be in a relationship and reluctance to tell adults what is going on. Adults in schools, homes, and churches have a responsibility to protect teenagers who are facing violence.

If our assumptions about love make controlling, possessive, jealous behavior seem normal, we need to change those assumptions. If our views of love condone violence against girls and women, we need to change those views.

LOVE THAT SACRIFICES

It makes sense that we find power in a love that is willing to make sacrifices. In so many ways, we live in a selfish culture, a place where people don't often give something up for someone else's sake. One of the reasons Twilight is compelling is that it shows a love that's very different from the bland me-first love we so often see. The love God promises us in Scripture is a love that sacrifices too, but sacrificial love in the Bible looks very, very different from Bella's self-erasing sacrifice.

Bella's sacrifice for Edward is *not* the compelling self-sacrifice that Christians learn about in Scripture. The model of Christian sacrifice is Jesus Christ. In 1 John 3:16, we know what love is because "Jesus Christ laid down his life for us," and this is our model for laying down our lives for others. In many ways, Bella's sacrifice is doable because she sees her life as so very trivial. In contrast, Jesus's sacrifice is of cosmic significance because of who He is as God. If we hope to imitate Christ's sacrifice, we cannot despise what we are sacrificing. This is especially true for women and girls in a culture that often subjects them to abuse and violence.

Christian self-sacrifice, particularly for women, is not about the erasure of a life for the sake of romance. It is about sharing the love and grace of Jesus Christ. Bella, despite Edward's many protests, is too reminiscent of so many women who have been counseled to suffer anything for the sake of a man, to accept abuse, to die for love.

Yes, real love makes sacrifices, but real love does not assume that the thing that is sacrificed has little worth. It doesn't seek pain for pain's sake or hide the truth of pain from a loved one. Real love, then, looks very different from Bella's love for Edward. Real love happens between two people of value, not between a girl who thinks she is nothing and the boy is everything.

A Different Kind of Love

The love in Twilight is also compelling because it is so serious. In our self-absorbed culture, we don't see much that is serious about love. So we enjoy reading Twilight because the love in the story is the opposite of the shallow loves that we know from television, movies, and life. It is the opposite of the random hookup, the false love that gets intimate one night and pretends nothing happened the next morning. Of course, we want a serious love.

Yet the serious love of Twilight is not a healthy love. It tries to find a center in another human being who cannot possibly be the center we need. It is open to danger, even to violence. Are we out of luck, then, if we want a serious love?

Thankfully, we are not. God provides us with a completely compelling, delightfully serious way of loving. God's kind of love is not bland and passionless. We read about it in 1 Corinthians 13:

> If I speak in the tongues of men and of angels, but have not love, I am only a resounding gong or a clanging cymbal. If I have the gift of prophecy and can fathom all mysteries and all knowledge, and if I have a faith that can move mountains, but have not love, I am nothing. If I give all I possess to the poor and surrender my body to the flames, but have not love, I gain nothing.
>
> Love is patient, love is kind. It does not envy, it does not boast, it is not proud. It is not rude, it is not self-seeking, it is not easily angered, it keeps no

record of wrongs. Love does not delight in evil but
rejoices with the truth. It always protects, always
trusts, always hopes, always perseveres.

Love never fails. (verses 1–8)

Now, *this* is a serious account of love. This is a love that is
central. This is a love that is beautiful. It challenges the selfishness and lack of seriousness of "love" in our me-first world, but
it does it in a different way than Bella and Edward do. This love
is not about becoming a satellite, orbiting around someone else,
yet it does protect and honor the loved one with all its might.
This love is not a love that destroys. This love builds up. This
kind of love cannot depend on another human being to give life
meaning, though it does greatly honor the people we love.

Or consider this passage about the magnitude of God's
love:

For I am convinced that neither death nor life,
neither angels nor demons, neither the present nor
the future, nor any powers neither height nor depth,
nor anything else in all creation, will be able to separate us from the love of God that is in Christ Jesus
our Lord. (Romans 8:38–39)

Of course we long for love, but the good news is that we
don't have to try desperately to find it from a human being.

Serious love, deep love, real love has been given to us in Jesus, and nothing can tear us out of His arms. He is a center that will not disappoint.

✝ THINK ABOUT IT/TALK ABOUT IT

1. What do you want from love?
2. Is there a part of you that thinks "real" love acts jealous and controlling?
3. Where do we get our ideals about love? From media, books, family?
4. What aspects of love, as described in the Bible, are most compelling to you?
5. Love doesn't allow for violence or abuse. If you or someone you know is a victim of dating or marriage violence, you need to be safe. Talk to an adult, friend, pastor, or teacher who can help. The National Coalition Against Domestic Violence has a Web site that will point you to resources that can help (www.ncadv.org).

Chapter 3

→>—<←

Body and Blood

Twilight's Take on Abstinence and Sex

THE TWILIGHT SAGA IS DRIVEN BY the unrelenting physical longing between Edward and Bella. Throughout the story, their sexual desire grows increasingly intense, but they wait until the night of their wedding to give in to that desire. Some Christian readers have celebrated the fact that they save sex for marriage, finding in their story an example of purity and self-control. But should Christian readers really be encouraged by the details of this story?

LIVING IN TENSION

The Twilight Saga covers a lot of pages, and the vast majority of those pages chronicle the sexual tension between Bella and Edward. Though they don't have sex until after their wedding in the fourth book, this doesn't mean that the first three books are any less about sexuality. The drama of the books hinges on the intensity of their physical reactions to one another. The books are charged with sexual feelings, and the overall effect of this electric charge is heightened by the anticipation—Bella's, Edward's, and the reader's—that is created by their choice to wait.

Meyer, of course, isn't the first author to write vampire stories, and vampire fiction has always been sexually charged. A vampire's thirst for blood, the very thing that defines him or her, is a symbol for sexuality. In Bram Stoker's *Dracula,* the threat of the vampire is a threat to an innocent girl, to her purity and goodness. Like in *Dracula,* Edward's deep thirst for Bella's blood is a metaphor for his sexual desire for her. "Which is tempting you more," Bella teases Edward, "my blood or my body?"[1]

Meyer gives this classic vampire theme a couple of interesting nuances. First, Edward's struggle with this desire is portrayed very dramatically. He's unlike vampires in other novels because he doesn't want to be a murderer and he wants to protect the innocence of the one he loves. He struggles with the threat he poses to Bella. In reading the books, we feel how very much Edward wants to bite her. We sense the danger involved in his desire even as we understand his determination to fight against it. Second, Bella fully returns Edward's desire. It is not

---

1. Stephenie Meyer, *New Moon* (New York: Little, Brown and Company, 2006), 52.

only that he wants her. She's a modern girl, and she isn't shy about wanting him in return.

Edward and Bella reverse some stereotypes. She is the one in the relationship constantly begging for more, the one pushing the boundaries. Edward continuously reestablishes those boundaries. Their choice to save sex for marriage is Edward's choice, not Bella's. Edward draws lines; Bella tries to blur them.

Because of the way Bella's blood calls out to him, Edward must constantly police his own desire and behavior. In drawing near to Bella, Edward "hesitated to test himself, to see if this was safe, to make sure he was still in control of his need."[2] Only then can he kiss her. His sexuality is charged with danger. Edward must constantly maintain his self-control, or he will stop being the good vampire Meyer has created and become the old threatening monster of other vampire stories.

Bella, though, takes little responsibility for her own self-control. All the hard work falls to Edward. Kissing him is too overwhelming. She forgets the danger and says her "will crumbled into dust the second our lips met."[3] He's frustrated with her for constantly challenging his restraint and chastises her for putting him through the pain of refusing her pleading. At one point, he has to ask her to stop taking off her clothes.

---

2. Stephenie Meyer, *Twilight* (New York: Little, Brown and Company, 2005), 282.
3. *New Moon*, 512.

Bella and Edward may be "waiting" for sex for most of their story, but reading the novels is still very much an erotic experience. Edward tells Bella, "Just because I'm resisting the wine doesn't mean I can't appreciate the bouquet."[4]

Delayed Gratification

Because of her commitment to the values of the Mormon faith, Meyer has stated publicly that she will not write about premarital sex. In the Twilight Saga, Bella and Edward wait for sex for a number of reasons. Edward, after all, is from another time. He is committed to the old-fashioned morality he has brought into the present from that day long ago when he was frozen in his perfect seventeen-year-old body. Twenty-first-century morality may not have much patience with delaying sexual gratification, but Edward holds on to his old-fashioned morals. He tells Bella, "I've stolen, I've lied, I've coveted...my virtue is all I have left."[5]

In reading, we participate in Bella's and Edward's longing for each other. For people who have grown up with the values of mainstream culture, their story of longing and waiting is surprising. In a world where it is rare to delay gratification, Edward and Bella represent a way of caring for each other outside the

---

4. *Twilight*, 306.
5. Stephenie Meyer, *Eclipse* (New York: Little, Brown and Company, 2007), 454.

norm. In a world where all responsibility for restraint and self-control is often placed on women, reading about a man willing to step out of his selfishness and practice restraint is surprising and intriguing.

For people who've grown up in communities that teach sexual abstinence outside of marriage, this story of waiting for sex in the midst of intense anticipation is very familiar and oddly contemporary. In such communities, there is plenty of sexual tension. Christians committed to saving sex for marriage experience the difficulty that comes with waiting and can recognize themselves in Edward and Bella. These communities are also full of people who know what it is to constantly push against boundaries and to have sexual tension heightened even as sexual experience is delayed. The heightened tension widespread among Christian youth is reflected in the common question, "How far is too far?" and the way that Christian couples who are "waiting" so often push boundaries to the breaking point.

This is one of the reasons we should be careful about seizing on the Twilight Saga as a story that provides a positive example for people committed to sexual abstinence and to purity. While Edward and Bella wait for marriage, they wait in a way that is all too common among Christians. As they wait, they allow the tension between them to build. They encourage that tension to build. They push borders and boundaries, and they create a situation in which they're always longing for more than they can or ought to have. This is the way most Christian couples wait, engaging in all kinds of sexual activities while trying desperately to save intercourse for marriage.

Several things in Bella and Edward's relationship encourage anguished desire instead of freedom from temptation. They've cut themselves off from people who can help them. Bella doesn't want to discuss sex with her parents. Edward's family surely would have been glad to help him with his struggles for self-control, but the couple cut themselves off from the support of friends and family. They are constantly alone together and spend nights alone in Bella's room. This kind of isolation and lack of support is a recipe for temptation.

Christians need to rethink our models of dating and of waiting. Instead of desperately holding out, we need to find ways to protect ourselves from the temptations created by the kind of waiting Bella and Edward engage in. Waiting in tension makes waiting more difficult, and frankly, it often becomes a wasted effort. We need to find ways to practice sexual abstinence outside of marriage that don't make us subject to the kind of anguished heightened anticipation that marks Bella and Edward's relationship before marriage. Instead of asking, "How far is too far?" we need to be accountable to one another and encourage each other to truly live in the story of goodness and faithfulness that God gives us to help us understand sexuality.

FAITHFULNESS

Bella and Edward don't have very convincing reasons to support their efforts to wait for sex. Edward waits because he is "old-fashioned." I doubt this reason captures your imagination. It may be nice to think about those chivalrous, old-fashioned values, but in the face of desire, I don't believe that just wanting to be old-fashioned will help anyone resist sexual temptation.

Christians have much more powerful reasons than being old-fashioned for insisting that sex belongs within marriage. Christians' belief that sex belongs within marriage is not because we are old-fashioned. We believe sex belongs within marriage because God wants good things for us. Sexuality is part of the compelling story of God's faithfulness to us, His people. God is faithful to Israel. Christ is faithful to the church.

Bella gets much closer to the point when she thinks about sex after her marriage: "How did people do this—swallow all their fears and trust someone else so implicitly with every imperfection and fear they had—with less than the absolute commitment that Edward had given me?"[6] In Bella's thinking, knowledge, trust, and commitment make sex possible. She acknowledges the intense vulnerability that is part of sexuality

---

6. Stephenie Meyer, *Breaking Dawn* (New York: Little, Brown and Company, 2008), 83.

and realizes that her marriage to Edward, their "absolute commitment" to each other, provides a safe, trustworthy context for that kind of vulnerability. Bella implies that sex could not have been good outside of marriage, hinting at the ways sexual purity is a gift.

Christians also believe that sex belongs within marriage because marriages ought to be a beautiful reflection of God's love for us and faithfulness to us. In several places in Scripture, sexual faithfulness in marriage is used as an image for the way God loves us. Hosea's story teaches us about God's faithfulness by showing an example of unfaithfulness. God tells the prophet Hosea to marry a woman who is a prostitute. Hosea takes "an adulterous wife and children of unfaithfulness, because the land is guilty of the vilest adultery in departing from the LORD" (Hosea 1:2). Hosea marries Gomer, and his faithful love for her, even in the face of her unfaithfulness, is a living picture of God's redeeming love. Hosea loves his unfaithful wife the way God loves us even though we chase after all kinds of things that are not God. Even though we are unfaithful, God promises steadfast love and mercy.

Human beings are the unfaithful ones in this story, but God is steadfast and true. God doesn't expect us to remain unfaithful though. God's transforming power allows us to lead a different kind of life, and faithful Christian marriage is one image of that kind of life. If we look at the picture of God's love that we see in the story of Hosea and Gomer, we see that waiting for sex until marriage is not just some arbitrary rule. Instead, it's a beautiful image of the faithfulness God shows to us and the way God can turn us into people who reflect His own faithful way of loving.

In a world full of unfaithfulness, faithfulness is an amazing witness to who God is and what God can do. We live in a world full of constant choices. Do I want the navy shoes or the gray ones? The pepperoni pizza or the veggie special? Will I take the elective in advanced chemistry, or should I have fun in an art class? We make endless choices, and we encourage even little children to express their personal preferences about all kinds of things. They can choose the french fries or the fruit, for instance, to go with their fast-food kids' meal. We can constantly update our "favorites" on our Facebook profile page or rearrange what we want to watch next on our Netflix queue.

Though it's difficult for people who've always had so many choices to imagine, not every society has so much pressure to choose. When I was living in Kenya, I remember the confused look on a friend's face when I asked her what her favorite food was. In a village where nearly everyone ate maize and beans 99 percent of the time, my question didn't make any sense. Food, for my friend, was not about preference. She wanted to know not about my *favorite* food, but about what the *staple* food was where I came from. For her, food was about survival, not choice. Her world didn't include the daily pressure to pick favorites, and she certainly wouldn't have defined herself by her favorite food or band or brand of jeans.

All the choices we have in our culture aren't necessarily a bad thing—they can be a lot of fun. But living in a world of endless choice does create a certain mind-set in us. We think that we are what we choose, and we're constantly on the look-out for a different choice, a better choice. We're free to be fickle, to want the newest update. We're perfectly willing to choose a new favorite food if something tastier than yesterday's favorite comes along.

This means we live in a condition where being faithful isn't something we're particularly used to. We're used to moving on to whatever is newer and better, not staying put and loving what was old and good. We're used to consumer choices, and it isn't too much of a stretch to go from choosing a favorite food or a favorite movie to choosing a new favorite person to love.

And people do choose new favorites. Faithfulness to one's love is a rare thing in our world. So many marriages end in divorce. Many people move through a series of loves as they go through life.

In such a world, faithfulness is a dramatic witness to the beautiful love of God. And not having sex if you are not married is a dramatic kind of faithfulness. In practicing sexual purity out-side of marriage, Christians are making a gigantic statement about what faithfulness looks like inside of marriage.

In Ephesians 5, Paul talks about the "mystery" in which the union between a husband and wife is an image of the union between Christ and the church. Earlier in that same chapter, Paul asks his readers to "Be imitators of God…and live a life of love, just as Christ loved us and gave himself up for us as a fragrant offering and sacrifice to God" (verses 1–2). Part of living that life of God involves the reminder that, among God's people, "there must not be even a hint of sexual immorality, or of any kind of impurity, or of greed, because these are improper for God's holy people" (verse 3). Sexual purity and faithfulness are God's good gifts to us, and they are powerful ways we can imitate God's love in this world.

DONE WAITING

In *Breaking Dawn*, the tensions of the saga are finally resolved. Bella and Edward are married at his family home. It's a fairy tale wedding, and Bella even wears an old-fashioned wedding dress to match Edward's old-fashioned tastes. We know the marriage means that Edward will finally transform her from human to vampire. She'll become like him.

First, though, she wants to consummate their marriage while she is yet human. Though she has longed through the whole story to leave her human life behind, Bella doesn't want to give up sex as a human experience. She marries Edward while still human and is determined to have her wedding night as a human bride. Since Meyer's vampires are insanely strong, this is an incredibly dangerous plan.

The account of their wedding night is a memorable one. Meyer avoids physical details, but that doesn't mean the telling won't draw the reader in. The wedding night is painted with both deep intimacy and fierce intensity. Both bride and groom are nervous, and we're reminded of Bella's fragility and humanity when she needs some time to clean up after the long journey to the honeymoon paradise. Edward gives her this time with the teasing words, "Don't take too long, Mrs. Cullen."[7] Instead of giving the details of what happens next, Meyer lets readers know that Bella felt like her skin was in flames and that Edward, in an effort to control the intensity of the moment, bit a pillow and destroyed the headboard. When they wake in the morning, the room is full of feathers from the pillow he destroyed.

Edward is horrified to discover that his bride has been injured. She downplays the bruises that cover her body, but Edward is incredibly angry with himself for having agreed to the plan. "Did you expect this, Bella?" he yells at her. "Were you anticipating that I would hurt you? Were you thinking it would be worse? Do you consider the experiment a success because you can walk away from it? No broken bones—that equals a victory?"[8]

---

7. *Breaking Dawn,* 81.
8. *Breaking Dawn,* 92.

Bella's new husband refuses to share her bed and injure her further. Again, we find Bella begging for more. She keeps at it, and he eventually surrenders. Sex is something so powerful that they both ignore the danger. Sex is portrayed as intimate, intense, and dangerous. Edward is right to be horrified that Bella has been injured. God intends sex to be loving and mutual, never a violent experience.

If you, like many readers, find these scenes exciting, it may be because it's part of a powerful cultural tradition in which sex is seen as dangerous, especially for women, and the excitement and intensity of sex is heightened by that sense of danger. We have to reject these lies. Sex is exciting—not because of danger, but because it's a gift from God.

In a marriage in which both husband and wife are committed to Jesus's command to love your neighbor as yourself, sex is not a threat to the wife. It's a terrible shame if this wedding night story serves to glorify violent sex or to suggest that sex should involve danger if it is to be intense and exciting. This dishonors a gift that God intends for good, turning it into something hurtful.

Later in *Breaking Dawn,* Edward and Bella's sexual relationship continues to show the reader the intensity and excitement between them. After Bella becomes a vampire, her physical relationship with Edward no longer poses a danger. Human sex, it seems, is nothing compared to vampire sex. Bella muses that "it didn't feel like I was ever going to find a point where I would think, *Now I've had enough for one day.* I was always going to want more."[9] Because they don't have to sleep, vampires have a lot of free time. The other couples in the Cullen family spend their nights having sex. His lack of a partner before Bella explains why Edward had so much time to study and practice the piano. Edward's brother Emmett teases Bella and Edward for failing to get wild enough to reduce their house to dust. Married vampire sex is about never-ending pleasure.

A GOOD GIFT

Sex is a good gift from God. In the Old Testament, the book Song of Songs uses erotic language to talk about the love between God and God's people and about human love. In Song of Songs, sexual love is portrayed as both beautiful and happy. Bible scholar Ellen Davis points out that the book shows human sexual love "in full mutuality and equality of status."[10] Sex is not portrayed as something dangerous. It is not a matter of one person having power over another. Instead, it is about a self-giving that goes both ways.

In recent years, churches have made great efforts to remind people that sex is not a bad thing. In a sinful world, sex is often associated with problems: people have sex with people they

---

9. *Breaking Dawn,* 483.
10. Ellen F. Davis, *Getting Involved with God: Rediscovering the Old Testament* (Cambridge, MA: Cowley Publications, 2001), 68.

shouldn't, at times that they shouldn't, in ways that don't reflect mutual love and self-giving. But the fact that in a sinful world sex sometimes comes with problems does *not* mean sex is bad. Sex is a gift from God created by God for God's good purposes. It is a witness to God's love and faithfulness in the world. It unites couples, bringing closeness, intimacy, and fun along with it. It is the way God has given us to bring children into the world. Churches have tried to recover the truth that sex is a good gift from God in order to free people from thinking that this gift is somehow shameful. Married people have been encouraged to enjoy the fullness of this gift.

Sex is a very good gift, but sex is not, as for Bella and Edward, merely about endless pleasure. Edward and Bella defer that pleasure, to be sure, but at the end of the day, their sexuality is only about one another. I see this often in Christians who are determined to wait until they marry to enjoy the goods of sexuality but who then picture sexuality as being ultimately about personal pleasure.

I am glad that Christians are now being told that sex is a gift from God, but I fear for people who picture marriage as an endless pleasure party. Sex in the Twilight Saga fits together perfectly with the fantasy that marriage is about limitless indulgence. But if we buy into this fantasy, if we believe married sex should look like it does for the vampires in the Twilight Saga, we will be stung and stunned when we experience the realities of daily life and commitment. Sex in marriage is about the inevitable give-and-take of two sinful people trying to love and be faithful to each other through all kinds of difficulties. I fear for young Christian parents, trained to look forward to a marriage of unadulterated sensuality, when toddlers wake them up at night, leaving them tired and cranky. I fear for young couples who have to deal with sexual brokenness or the trauma of past abuse that can make it very difficult to enjoy the goods of married sexuality. Married sex is a good gift indeed, but it is not the whole of married life.

Even in marriage, sex can all too easily become selfish. Yet God designed sex to work against our tendency to selfishness. At its best, God's good gift of sexuality takes a person and pulls him or her out of selfishness. Sex is not supposed to be a me-first indulgence. It ought to help a married couple pay attention to each other instead of living in self-absorption. For a couple who hope for their marriage to be centered on Jesus Christ, sexuality ought to turn them away from caring about only themselves and their own family and turn them instead toward loving and serving God. Sexuality is God's good gift, but it is not finally about self-satisfaction. Sexuality is for the glory of God.

✝ THINK ABOUT IT/TALK ABOUT IT

1. Do you have someone you can talk with honestly about the way "waiting" for sex does or doesn't

happen for you and your friends? How can we find ways to wait that don't increase temptation?

2. Describe God's faithful love. How is sexual purity a witness to God's faithfulness?

3. Reflect on Bella's feelings about the connections between vulnerable intimacy and lifelong commitment. How can intimacy without commitment cause pain?

4. Do you agree that faithfulness is rare in our culture? Who has been an example of faithfulness in your life?

5. What are your expectations, whether you're married or not, for sex within marriage? Do you expect perfection? Do you see sex as fearful or shameful? What are the good things about married life that look different from the picture of endless and intense sex we get from movies or married vampires?

6. What messages about sexuality have you gotten from church, family, friends, and society? Is sex seen as something good? as something shameful?

Chapter 4

✦►◄✦

The Superhero and the Girl Next Door

Gender Roles in Twilight

THE TWILIGHT SAGA CONTAINS interesting assumptions about what it means to be masculine and feminine. It's full of characters who represent ideal and not-so-ideal males and females, and it challenges some of our assumptions about what is masculine and what is feminine. It also reinforces some stereotypes about those same assumptions.

The questions we've already discussed—questions about romance, love, and sexuality—are intimately tied to our ideas about what it means to be male and female. Many of the problems that come from certain beliefs about romance, love, and sexuality are connected to ideas about what it means to be male and female that are themselves troublesome. Both male and female readers may see themselves in the characters of the saga, and it's all too easy to measure ourselves or other people by the standards portrayed in the novels.

Bella is a girl-next-door heroine. She's competent but also full of self-doubt. Edward is Bella's indestructible protector. What do their characters have to say about what it means to be created male or female?

AN ORDINARY GIRL

Readers identify with Bella because she's an everygirl. "I'm absolutely ordinary," Bella insists, "well, except for bad things like all the near-death experiences and being so clumsy that I'm almost disabled."[1] Many of us can relate to Bella's feelings. She is ordinary, normal, nothing outside the box. At the same time, she regrets her deficiencies. She's incredibly awkward and gets into accident after accident.

There are two sides to Bella—she is both strong and weak. On one hand, she's unusually competent. She can run a household better than most adults I know, and she's extraordinarily self-reliant. At the same time, her clumsiness and poor judgment come together to create conditions in which she often needs to be rescued. In general, Bella is much more aware of her weakness than she is of her strength. The most

---

1. Stephenie Meyer, *Twilight* (New York: Little, Brown and Company, 2005), 210.

obvious feature of her character is that she puts herself down at every turn.

Her self-consciousness about her clumsiness means she won't dance—she's horrified at the thought of the prom. As a rule, she doesn't want special attention of any kind, fearing that such attention will only highlight her weaknesses. While her strong attachment to Edward is the main reason she is so determined to become a vampire, she is also drawn to vampire life because it promises her the opposite of all her human weaknesses. In *New Moon,* she explains that "more than anything, I wanted to be fierce and deadly, someone no one would dare mess with."[2]

Though Edward's feelings for Bella are undeniably strong, though he loves her deeply, he also tends to focus on her weakness. In part, this is less about Bella herself and more about the fact that he has fallen in love with a human being, and to him, to be human is to be weak. Edward thus emphasizes Bella's fragility, the ways that she is constantly in danger just because she is human. It is not only being human that makes Bella vulnerable though. Edward agrees with Bella's own estimation of herself—she is particularly prone to danger. Edward, then, acts as her protector because, he says, Bella is "one of those people who just attract accidents like a magnet."[3] Edward also believes

---

2. Stephenie Meyer, *New Moon* (New York: Little, Brown and Company, 2006), 263.

3. *Twilight,* 109.

that Bella is vulnerable because she is so desirable. Her very attractiveness makes her a target for trouble. Edward tries to challenge Bella's more negative views of herself, but it's also probable that the overprotectiveness and concern for her weakness that dominate his interactions with her add to her sense that she isn't very strong. As readers, we believe that Bella is an everygirl because she tells us it's true. We also believe it because this is the main thing we know about her; in other ways, her character is left largely undrawn. Like Bella, we all have strength and weakness, and we're likely to be familiar with her worries about her weakness.

EXTRAORDINARY GIRLS

Edward's beautiful sisters, Rosalie and Alice, represent, to Bella, a contrast to her own ordinariness. Alice and Rosalie are poised, gorgeous, gifted, and powerful. Bella sees herself as clumsy, ordinary, average, and weak. These vampire sisters possess female beauty that goes beyond anything a supermodel on a magazine cover could ever boast.

In their differences from Bella, the characters of Alice and Rosalie embody different aspects of what it means to be female. If Bella is the self-deprecating girl-next-door, Alice and Rosalie are ideals of different ways of being a girl, ideals that Bella can't imagine ever achieving.

Bella has two very different relationships with Alice and with Rosalie. Almost from the beginning, she and Alice recognize each other as sisters and form a close friendship. In contrast, the relationship between Rosalie and Bella is filled with tension.

Alice is small, dark haired, and fiery. Unlike most members of the Cullen family, Carlisle didn't transform her from human to vampire. Alice remembers very little of her human life. Her sad and unclear past includes being committed to an asylum because she had premonitions—the human talent that would become her vampire gift. She was transformed by an asylum keeper but left to make her own way as a vampire. Wanting something different than the violent vampire life, she found her partner, Jasper, and together they joined the Cullen family.

For many vampires in the Twilight Saga, some talent from their human lives is brought forward into their vampire lives and strengthened into a unique gift. Alice's gift is an ability to see the future. It's not a fail-safe ability, because the future changes when people's decisions change, but it is of great benefit to her family.

Alice has fun with typically girlie activities—shopping, fashion, and party planning—and she's determined to enjoy these things in her friendship with Bella even though they aren't Bella's preferred forms of fun. Alice plans fancy parties and an elaborate wedding for Bella. After Edward and Bella marry, she stocks Bella's closet with a dream wardrobe.

She is very much a sympathetic sister to Bella. She's there for her for fun and as a confidante, and she's also incredibly powerful. Alice is vital to Bella's last-minute rescue of Edward from his attempt at self-destruction in *New Moon*. She also uses her gifts and strengths to play an important role in saving Edward and Bella's daughter and the Cullen family from the Volturi threat at the end of *Breaking Dawn*.

Rosalie was an astonishingly beautiful human being, and her beauty has been carried forward and heightened in her vampire life, making her unimaginably stunning. She is hostile to Bella from the very start and often expresses her disapproval over Bella's relationship with her brother. She is responsible in *New Moon* for misinforming Edward about Bella's death and sending him on his death quest to Italy.

Rosalie's sad human story is one in which she lived a shallow life, spoiled and petted for her beauty. While she was drawn to the real, loving relationships she saw in the life of a friend with a husband and baby, she was engaged to a man who prized her only for her beauty. One night, her cruel fiancé and his friends raped and beat her. Carlisle found her on the brink of death and transformed her into a vampire. The beautiful vampire Rosalie took her revenge on her attackers. She killed them, but she did not drink their blood.

Until we learn her story, Rosalie is an unsympathetic character in the saga—a cold and heartless beauty. The revealing of her past, though, also reveals something of her current motivations. She wishes, above all else, to protect her family, and she sees Bella as a threat to their security.

Later, when confronted with Bella's determination to become a vampire, Rosalie is angered by her choice. "You already have everything," Rosalie tells Bella. "You have a whole life ahead of you—everything I want. And you're going to just throw it all away. Can't you see that I'd trade everything I have to be you? You have the choice that I didn't have, and you're choosing wrong!"[4] Rosalie regrets the shallowness and tragedy of her human life. She wishes for the human experiences of a true, loving relationship and, most of all, for motherhood.

Alice embodies the feminine ideals of spunk, energy, and girliness. She's the perfect girlfriend and sister, and she's also incredibly powerful and isn't afraid to use her power. Rosalie embodies other aspects of what it means to be an ideal women. Her femininity is shown in her commitment to her family and in her desire to be a mother. For Bella, both are impossible ideals, images of the kind of perfect girl she thinks she can never be. As pictures of what being a woman is all about, Bella, Alice, and Rosalie represent different facets of the ideals of our culture. The three characters reinforce some stereotypes while bringing others into question.

---

4. Stephenie Meyer, *Eclipse* (New York: Little, Brown and Company, 2007), 166.

Meaning of a Girl's Life

While Bella is an "ordinary" heroine, she does defy a lot of stereotypes about what it means to act feminine. It is Alice who loves clothes and parties and Rosalie whose dreams center on marriage and babies. Bella is a jeans and T-shirt kind of girl who has been taught that it's dangerous to focus all her dreams on marrying Prince Charming.

Yet in one very worrisome way, Bella falls right into stereotypes about what it means to be female: she's willing to erase herself for the sake of Edward. Her life is completely subsumed by his, and she has no interests or hobbies outside of him. Going to college is her plan B; it's a distant second to what she really wants—a future that's all about Edward.

In some ways, this works in the books to allow lots of readers to identify with Bella. If the main thing we know about her character is that she cares about love, almost all of us can imagine ourselves in her shoes. If she were a more defined character in other ways, if she spent tons of energy on soccer or indie music or giggling with friends, it would certainly change the story in ways that would make it harder for so many readers to identify with her. Not everyone cares about soccer, after all, but most people care about love.

But Bella's self-erasure is terrifying. Erasing the self is a real problem for girls and women in our society. While little girls tend to have many interests, to speak up confidently in class, and to feel comfortable putting themselves forward, older girls often get the message that they ought to step back, take themselves out of the limelight, and make some more room for the boys. Older girls and women, then, often feel that they've lost their voices in the world. It gets difficult to speak up, and sometimes it gets difficult even to know who we are. It's not uncommon for women to feel that somewhere along the way they've lost themselves.

Lots of girls and women have mixed feelings about our cultural ideas of what it means to be feminine. Bella's story picks up on those mixed feelings. On one hand, she's not a typical girlie-girl. She doesn't have much interest in the perfect prom dress, for instance, and in this she defies easy stereotypes about what it means to be female. On the other hand, Bella's character lets readers embrace the common feeling that love is incredibly important and that, just maybe, total self-reliance isn't all it's cracked up to be. Bella's a powerful girl in many ways, but there's something compelling—and disturbing—about her need for Edward.

What it means to be female isn't an easy question. Most of us feel tension here. Maybe we, like Alice, *like* traditional girlie things and enjoy lipstick and dressing up. Maybe we don't. Or, like Rosalie, maybe family and motherhood are a huge part of the way we hope to live our lives as women. This isn't true for all women though; maybe family is much less important to your sense of what it means to be female and love God. Maybe some other passion or talent is the stuff you dream about. Girliness and maternal feelings aren't bad, but they're not all that there is to being a woman created in God's image.

Maybe, like Bella, your sense of being feminine isn't particularly about girliness or maternal feelings. In Bella's character, though, I wish there were another passion or talent important to her ideas about what a happy life is all about. Losing ourselves to a boy or a man, erasing our personalities and interests and goals, is a huge problem, a danger that damages lots of lives. If Bella's story makes it seem like a happy life is best found in losing all the things that make us who we are, then we need to think twice about her story.

I don't mean to suggest that happiness is all about "being yourself" or that we should put the happiness of our individual selves above the good of existing in relationships and communities. But part of what makes relationships and communities fun and interesting and good is that they're full of people with passions and talents, people who want to use those passions and talents *for* each other and for the good of the whole. If we flatten ourselves, erasing our personalities, we bring nothing to a relationship or a community.

STRONG PROTECTORS

In Bella's eyes, Edward is all a man ever could be. While she is ordinary, he is beyond extraordinary. He's her ideal. Bella says,

"I wasn't interesting. And he was. Interesting…and brilliant… and mysterious…and perfect…and beautiful…and possibly able to lift full-sized vans with one hand."[5] Edward is a knight in shining armor, a perfect superhero. While snuggling up to Edward, Bella compares him to Michelangelo's statue of *David*, "except this perfect marble creature wrapped his arms around me to pull me closer."[6]

All through the Twilight Saga, Edward protects Bella from her own clumsiness and stupidity and from the various monsters who want to destroy her. Edward says that protecting her has become "a full-time occupation that requires my constant presence."[7] Edward is a leader; he's the responsible one in the relationship, the one who takes on the tasks of maintaining Bella's safety. He's a fearsome hunter, a loyal brother and son, and commands his dark urges with formidable self-control. Edward is the dangerous bad boy who is attractive because he is supposed to be off-limits, and, of course, he's incredibly gorgeous.

We can't discuss the male characters in the Twilight Saga without paying attention to Jacob Black. Bella's close friendship with Jacob isn't normal for her. While she usually holds people at a distance, she and Jacob spend happy hours together, getting to know one another well, and their friendship becomes

---

5. *Twilight*, 79.
6. *Eclipse*, 439.
7. *Twilight*, 211.

truly intimate. Jacob is characteristically happy; he's big and strong, warm and safe.

While Jacob and Edward are presented in contrast to each other, they share a number of attractive characteristics, characteristics the series suggests are typically male. Both boys, after all, are something out of the ordinary. Both are supernatural creatures, heroes with enormous amounts of power. Jacob, like Edward, is a natural leader. Both are incredibly attractive, and both would do anything for Bella. Both boys, too, are ready to do battle against any enemy who threatens Bella, who thinks this is a natural male trait, saying, "The urge to fight must be a defining characteristic of the Y chromosome. They were all the same."[8]

The two extraordinary boys fight over the ordinary girl. "She is mine," Edward tells his rival with resolve. "I didn't say I would fight fair."[9] There is a particularly charged scene in *Eclipse* in which Jacob, radiating werewolf heat, keeps Bella from freezing through the night. Edward, as a cold vampire, is fiercely jealous of Jacob's ability to provide the comfort, safety, and physical closeness Bella needs.

Jacob and Edward represent two possible paths Bella could take, but there is never a question of her going down a third path. She unequivocally rejects the attentions of her classmate Mike, a nice, ordinary boy who can't compete with two superheroes.

---

8. *Eclipse*, 463.
9. *Eclipse*, 341.

Mike's ordinariness makes him an afterthought in comparison to Jacob's and Edward's extraordinariness.

GREAT EXPECTATIONS

Edward is an impossible ideal. If we want boyfriends or husbands to look like Edward, we're demanding more from those boyfriends and husbands than anybody can or should give. Demanding that someone squeeze himself into an Edward mold would truly be a cruel requirement.

No real man is a marble statue of perfection. What's more, no real man *should* be. Part of the fun of loving someone is in loving him flaws and all. A perfect marble statue can't cry with you, or share your weakness for potato chips, or allow you to see if he is struggling or afraid. It's disturbing that Edward has to shoulder all the responsibility for self-control in the relationship. Reading the Twilight Saga, I want Bella to take some of that responsibility too.

Bella actually hints at this nicely when she explains that one of the reasons she longs to be transformed into a vampire is so she can stand on equal footing with Edward. In their marriage, perhaps, they can share responsibility in the way she imagines, when she says, "It just seems logical…a man and woman have to be somewhat equal…as in, one of them can't always be swooping in and saving the other one. They have to save each other equally."[10] In Bella and Edward's relationship, though, this problem of unequal footing is solved by her giving up her ordinary humanity. She becomes a superhero too. It's a fun story, but this misses the true beauty of human love stories in which two ordinary people make a go of it together despite not being perfect.

NOT-SO-SIMPLE STEREOTYPES

When thinking about what it means to be male and female, it's hard to avoid the various stereotypes we associate with the two. For example, we tend to believe that girls are emotional and boys are aggressive. Different products are advertised to girls and to boys. You can walk down the toy aisles of your local superstore, and it's easy to see which is the boy aisle and which aisle is stocked for girls. The girl aisle is full of bubblegum pink, princess dresses, and toys for playing house. The boy aisle has a nice selection of wheeled vehicles and action figures equipped for battle. Though the "toy aisles" for teens and adults aren't quite so obvious, things are still carefully marketed to the two genders.

While everyone knows it's not as simple as all that, we certainly have models about what normal—or even ideal—women and men should look like and act like. We say things

10. *Twilight,* 473.

like, "She's a girlie-girl," or "Boys will be boys," and everyone has a pretty good idea of what we mean by these expressions.

We dress baby girls in pink and baby boys in blue. Seems normal and natural, right? It's hard for us to imagine baby clothing any other way, and it seems particularly odd to think about putting a little boy in pink. This gender rule isn't natural though. That is, it doesn't follow from anything inherent in the way God created baby boys and girls. In the United States, pink and blue color norms for baby clothes didn't take root until the 1920s.[11] In fact, at the time, some people even argued that pink, as a strong, manly color, was obviously more appropriate for boys. The point of this example is that the things we assume are "natural" for boys and girls, like Bella's assumption that fighting must be characteristic of boys, aren't necessarily as natural and normal as we believe. And Christians have an especially good reason for raising this question.

As Christians, we learn from the Word of God that we have to be suspicious of the ways we tend to see things. We live in a sinful world, under a condition of sin, and sin influences our viewpoints. It affects our ability to see what is true and what is false. It affects our ability to distinguish between what is natural (as God intends it to be) and what is sinful (the way selfish human beings want it to be). Paul talks about this in the first chapter of Romans. Because of sin, human "thinking became

---

11. Jo B. Paoletti, "Clothing and Gender in America: Children's Fashions, 1890–1920," *Signs* 13: 1 (Autumn 1987), 136–43.

futile" and "foolish" human "hearts were darkened" (verse 21). God shows us how God intends things to be, but our ability to see those things clearly has been damaged by sin.

Sin messes up our way of looking at the world, which means we need to be suspicious of ourselves when we're convinced we know exactly how things ought to be. We need God to heal our abilities to see and know the world. Questions about women and men, about what it means to be male and female, are areas where we especially need to keep these two things in mind. Because being male and female is natural, because it's a basic part of who we are, we tend to think we get it. When we're overly confident, though, we're likely to be deceived.

Rules and ideals about what it means to be male and female have done a lot of damage in this world. For instance, ideals about thin female bodies are linked to anorexia and bulimia as well as to the feelings of self-loathing so many girls and women feel when comparing themselves to fashion models. Ideals about muscular male bodies are becoming more tyrannical too. Ideals about male power and female weakness are linked to violence against women and the choices of many women to act weak, step down, and let men take the spotlight. These are just a few examples of the ways that stereotypes hurt people and interfere with both men's and women's abilities to serve God with all that they are. If a woman or a man doesn't fit the mold for what people expect women and men to be, that person is often mocked or socially isolated.

The self-erasure we see in Bella is a harmful feminine stereotype, a result of sin and not of what God wants for girls. The crazy demand to be a superhero that we see in Edward and Jacob is a harmful masculine stereotype, a result of sin and not of what God wants for boys. As Christians seeking God's truth and asking Him to heal our ways of seeing and knowing, we want to look for God's perspective on what being male and female is all about. We can't just buy into stereotypes and assume they reflect God's will for our lives.

CREATED MALE AND FEMALE

If sin twists our ability to know what God wants for us as men and women, how can we hope to know God's good intentions for us? How can we hope to be godly men and women? Thankfully, we've been given a way to see what God's good intentions are through reading Scripture. God heals our brokenness and gives us the power of the Holy Spirit to help us live lives that match up with those good intentions.

The fact that God created us male and female (Genesis 1:27) is an important place for us to start. Though sinful eyes make it tough to see what God wants for us as male and female, we know from the very beginning of Scripture that the simple fact that we exist as male and female *is* God's intention, part of the good plan He has for us. It means that God created us to live with each other and to be different from one another.

Dangerous stereotypes are instruments of sin, but difference it-self is a good thing. God made us to be different from each other and to love and be there for each other through our dif-ferences. When God created us male and female, God looked at the situation and called it good (verse 31).

God's Word also gives us encouragement as we think about challenging the way stereotypes cause harm in our lives. When we look at the way Jesus lived His life as a man, we see that some of our worst stereotypes about what it means to be male must not be true. Jesus is a savior who chose to accept death on a cross. When Jesus was being arrested, one of His friends cut off the ear of a servant of the priest. Jesus told the man to "put your sword back in its place" (Matthew 26:52). This flies in the face of our assumption that boys have to love violence. Jesus also interacted with women in ways that surprised His friends. He treated women not as lesser beings, but as valued friends.

Paul affirms that what Jesus has done for us as Christians includes both men and women. So "there is neither Jew nor Greek, slave nor free, male nor female, for you are all one in Christ Jesus" (Galatians 3:28). When the Holy Spirit is poured out on God's people, Peter explains that a prophecy from the book of Joel is being fulfilled. "In the last days, God says, I will pour out my Spirit on all people. Your sons and daughters will prophesy, your young men will see visions, your old men will dream dreams. Even on my servants, both men and women, I will pour out my Spirit in those days, and they will prophesy" (Acts 2:17–18). Sons and daughters, men and women, male and female, all witness to God's power.

Figuring out how to love and give glory to God as the male and female people we are isn't easy. It's not as simple as saying, "Look, we're all the same; there shouldn't be any difference." After all, God created us this way. It's also not as simple as looking at the way "traditional" roles dictate that we live and assuming that "tradition" reflects God's will. After all, tradition may well be sinful.

We can work together, though, as sisters and brothers in Christ, to love and glorify God as we are created—male and female. We can work together to discover what that means, to challenge sinful assumptions, and to honor and care for each other in our differences. We can work together to learn from Scripture and from the Spirit's presence in our lives what it means to be who we are and to give glory to God.

⚱ THINK ABOUT IT/TALK ABOUT IT

1. Do you identify with certain characters in the Twilight Saga in the ways they live their lives as male and female?

2. How do characters in the books perpetuate gender stereotypes? How do they challenge those stereotypes?

3. How can stereotypes cause harm? Have you seen this in your life or in the life of a friend?

4. The concept of sin making it difficult to see what God intends for us is an important one. Brainstorm a list of things we tend to believe are "natural." Are they really natural? Do they reflect God's will as we see it in His Word?

5. How do you think about living as created male or female? How can we glorify God as girls and boys, men and women?

Chapter 5

->-<-

Baseball and Loyalty

Twilight and the Ideal Family

EDWARD'S PERFECT FAMILY, the opposite of her own, is a large part of Bella's love for him. Her family is broken. His family is loyal. Her family lets her down. His family would die to rescue her. The beautiful, eternal family of vampires stands in stark contrast to the ordinariness and weakness of Bella's parents, and she comes to cherish her relationship with them almost as much as she cherishes Edward.

It seems obvious that family is important to Christians. How, then, should Christians think through the different messages about family found in the Twilight Saga?

FAMILY DISAPPOINTS

Family in the Twilight world reflects the truth about family in the real world in one simple way: Family disappoints us. This is certainly the case when we think about Bella's family. Bella, like so many of us, is a child of divorce. Her mother isn't particularly reliable, while her father is rarely in touch. So Bella learns to rely on herself.

Before she meets Edward and his family, Bella is essentially alone in the world. She has no sisters or brothers. For all practical purposes, she is without parents.

Her mother, Renee, is kindly enough, but she isn't there for her daughter. She wants to travel with her new husband, and Bella moves in with her dad in the town of Forks in order to give her mother the freedom to do so. Thus Bella is alone at a vulnerable time. She is maturing, leaving girlhood behind and edging toward being a woman. At this crucial moment in her life, her mother effectively abandons her. Bella routinely hides things from her mother and treats her like an incompetent child. She can't count on her mother to provide protection or a listening ear.

Bella's father, Charlie, cares about his daughter, but he is inept and disappointing. Charlie spends most of his time away from the house. Just like with her mom, Bella takes the parental role in her relationship with him. When she moves in with him, Bella takes over the household cooking and duties. She competently whips up delicious dinners and makes sure both she and her father are well cared for. When he expresses concern about her, she tries to smooth over his worries and avoids serious conversations with him about sex.

Bella describes her new life with her dad as "like having my own place."[1] She enjoys this independence, but we get hints that even self-reliant Bella sometimes longs for more from her parents. When her dad shows concern for her, she tells us that her "throat suddenly felt tight. I wasn't used to being taken care of, and Charlie's unspoken concern caught me by surprise."[2] She's very self-reliant, but she's still touched when her dad reaches out to her.

Bella sometimes can't and sometimes won't rely on her parents for the things children, even nearly grown children, rightly rely on their parents for. In many ways, her parents are physically and emotionally absent, but she doesn't nurse bitterness against them. Instead, she treats them like the well-meaning and largely incompetent people they are.

They don't protect her. They can't. How can human parents protect a daughter from werewolves and vampires?

At every turn, though, Bella tries to protect them. One of her deepest worries about her involvement with Edward is that it will bring danger to her parents. When James tries to murder Bella, he lures Bella to him by threatening her mother. She willingly steps into danger for her mom's sake. When Bella becomes a vampire, she's afraid of hurting Charlie. She asks her new family to protect him.

---

1. Stephenie Meyer, *Twilight* (New York: Little, Brown and Company, 2005), 54.
2. *Twilight*, 54.

As readers, we relate to Bella. We relate because all of our families are disappointing. Parents fail to be consistent. They show their human weaknesses. Children fail to love their parents. All families make mistakes.

Some families are far more terrible than Bella's. Some parents grip their children so tightly that their control becomes oppressive. Much, much worse, some parents are abusive, emotionally or physically. Such families betray their children in the worst possible ways by injuring what they are supposed to protect, harming what they are supposed to nurture.

It's also the case that many families are much less disappointing than Bella's. Some readers of this book will think, *Hey, I have a fantastic family. They're there for me. We really love each other.* But even the most loving families disappoint. Even the most nurturing families are still, well, human. Parents are weak, ordinary people, and all of us, as we grow up, see the weakness and ordinariness in our parents in ways we might not have noticed in the second grade.

It makes sense that we identify with Bella's need for self-reliance. It also makes sense that we identify with her attraction to the Cullen family.

A Beautiful, Eternal Family

Edward's family appears in sparkling contrast to the shortcomings of Bella's own parents. His parents, Carlisle and Esme, are kind, wise, and caring. Unlike her broken family, they're also *together*. While Bella's parents divorced, Carlisle and Esme are knit together for eternity.

Carlisle is the "father" of this vampire family because he changed most of them into vampires. In the books, though, Meyer goes to great lengths to show that Carlisle's decision to transform them into vampires was not made lightly. He changed them only at moments when their deaths seemed otherwise certain. Vampire life, for almost all vampires besides the Cullens, is portrayed in the books as lonely and selfish. The Cullens are set apart from other vampires by their connection to and care for one another.

Edward also comes to Bella with a slew of gorgeous siblings—Rosalie and Emmett, Jasper and Alice. Not only are they beautiful; they're also great fun (wild game of baseball on a stormy night, anyone?). It's also nice that Alice's ability to predict the stock market provides them with more money than they could ever need.

The Cullens are fiercely loyal to one another. Meyer portrays their family relationship with a great deal of charm. The siblings support each other but also playfully tease each other. These vegetarian vampires are willing to die for one another without missing a beat. They're incredibly gifted, and they're immortal. The precious bond they have will never be broken. Here, in so many ways, is the ideal family—the family Bella never had.

Bella's grief over losing Edward dominates the story in *New Moon.* It's important that this grief is not for Edward alone. Bella feels like she has died because "it had been more than just losing the truest of true loves, as if that were not enough to kill anyone. It was also losing a whole future, a whole family—the whole life that I'd chosen."[3] So much of Bella's attraction to Edward is tied up with her attraction to his family. Despite her self-reliance, she longs to be part of this close-knit group. Once they see what she means to Edward, the Cullens adopt Bella unreservedly. They shower her with warmth and consideration, with gifts and parties. She becomes one of them.

At the end of *Breaking Dawn,* it is their unique bond as a family that saves the Cullens from the massive threat posed by the Volturi. The bonds of family in this universe run deep and strong. They are unbreakable. As the Cullens prepare for their showdown with the Volturi, they are motivated by the desire to save their family. They work tirelessly to keep one another safe.

Bella's gift as a "shield" makes her impervious to attacks from other vampires' powers. Edward cannot read her thoughts, and the torturing Volturi cannot throw her to the ground in pain. This gift, though, becomes most valuable when Bella learns to extend it. She learns to cast her shield outward so that it protects those she loves. The shield is most important

---

3. Stephenie Meyer, *New Moon* (New York: Little, Brown and Company, 2006), 398.

when it becomes a shield of defense, not for only Bella, but also for her family.

Think about the difference between the red-eyed Volturi and the golden-eyed Cullens. It isn't only that one group is immoral and the other moral, one wicked and the other good. Neither is it simply that one group lives in violence, without mercy, sustained by cold-blooded murder while the other is bonded together by their "vegetarian" choice to live in peace.

No, the key difference between the two groups is that one is a coven while the other is a *family*.

MORMON FAMILY HOPE

In many ways, the Cullen family reflects the hopes of the author's Mormon faith. For Mormons, *eternal hope* is linked with family. Mormons believe that the family unit will last for all of eternity.

There is a crucial difference between this belief and the usual Christian expectation that we will know and be reunited with people we love in the kingdom of God. For Mormons, the family structure remains the basic unit of eternity. Salvation happens in, through, and for families. Eternal life is family life, continuous with family life as it is known here and now. People become holy through a good family life. A Mormon marriage is believed to be for both time (this life) and eternity (forever). This is the reason Mormons are interested in studying their family trees. Mormon families want to find out who among their ancestors didn't know about the Mormon faith. They provide baptism for these dead family members in the hope of strengthening their eternal families.

Families aren't important just for eternal hope though. Hope for Mormons *in this life* is also pinned on the family. Family life is supposed to provide everything Bella doesn't get from Charlie and Renee—stability, protection, and happiness. The Mormon family is supposed to be moral and affect society for the better. God is understood to bless faithful families.

The Mormon church distributes free literature printed with rosy, glowing images of family life. Beautiful and happy children gather around tables filled with food. Mom and Dad are together, smiling, generous, and kind. Everyone is smartly dressed, neatly brushed, attractive. Family members touch each other affectionately, casually. The pictures show families that are the opposite of the disappointment we all have known in our own families.

When we think about family in Twilight, then, two very different things are going on. On one side, Meyer captures the fragility of real human families. Our families are ordinary, weak, and disappointing. As we get older, we often realize this in new ways, ways difficult for us to accept. We realize, like Bella, that the families we grew up in can't protect us from everything or meet all our needs.

On the other side, Meyer offers a glittering image of a family that won't disappoint. The Cullens are a family in which happiness and togetherness can be realized, a family that can "save" Bella from her mortal life.

GOD'S PERSPECTIVE ON WEAK AND ORDINARY THINGS

How should Christians think about these two images of family? Let's begin with the weakness of our ordinary families. Even if we try to act otherwise, we all know that families are flawed. What do we do with those flaws? How do we live with them?

We get a hint from Scripture when Paul talks about weakness. When he wrote to the church in the city of Corinth, Paul wanted folks to see that God's view of weak and ordinary things is not always what we might expect. In 1 Corinthians 1:27–29, Paul lets his readers know: "God chose the foolish things of the world to shame the wise; God chose the weak things of the world to shame the strong. He chose the lowly things of this world and the despised things—and the things that are not—to nullify the things that are, so that no one may boast before him."

In fact, God uses weak things in a special way and acts in ways we don't expect. Specifically, God acted by becoming human for us. Being human is a weak thing, but God entered into this mess with us to show us how much He cares. We read in the first chapter of the gospel of John that "The Word became flesh and made his dwelling among us. We have seen his glory…" (verse 14).

All through history, people have wondered how something so strange, so weak, could be true. How could a majestic and mysterious God become human? How could the holy God of Israel be born and cry, have ten fingers and toes, or enjoy a fish dinner? We're talking about a God who is so glorious and tremendous that people knew better than to even say His name out loud. How could a God like that be known the way Jesus's friends and disciples knew Him? God in the flesh seems weak and foolish. Flesh is as weak as it gets, after all. Flesh disappoints. It betrays us. Being flesh means we suffer and die.

Paul wants us to recognize how fabulous this is. While it seems like a contradiction to believe that the powerful Creator of the universe came to us as a tiny baby, Paul positively glories in this. It *is* astounding that God would become flesh, which makes it all the more wonderful, all the more full of grace. God chose the weak things of the world to shame the strong. God is in no danger of being damaged by dwelling fully with us in our weakness.

The incarnation of Jesus is *the* shining example of how God gives us good gifts in the middle of weak, ordinary life.

Christian thinkers have often taken another step here. If God is so good as to join us in the middle of our human mess, then this should change the way we deal with the mess.

Because God jumped into our mess, our weakness, we have to approach that mess differently. We can look at our limits, and instead of figuring that we'd better work hard to overcome those limits, we can think about the sweet gifts God gives us in the middle of weakness and limitation. Yes, we are weak and ordinary. But Jesus jumped into that weakness and ordinariness with us. That means we can find God's gifts in the middle of everyday, ordinary life.

We don't have to have "perfect," ideal families for our homes to be places where God can do good work. Our families don't have to be beautiful, well-scrubbed, always smiling folks constantly ready to be photographed for the cover of some magazine called *Your Perfect Life Today.* This doesn't mean it's all right for our parents to hurt us or for us to hurt our children or brothers or sisters. It does mean, though, that God loves ordinary, everyday people—people who fail each other and disappoint each other.

The truth is that being a family is hard. Living with other people is hard. Sometimes it's relatively easy to be kind—or at least to tolerate—people at work or school. After all, we only have to see those people for a few hours at a stretch. But you can't escape family. You have to see them each and every day. You have to share the bathroom and the kitchen. Every single day, you notice if they leave toothpaste in the sink or eat the last bagel, the one you wanted for breakfast. If a family member gets sick, another family member will take care of her. Have you ever changed a diaper or cleaned up after a sick child? Have you figured out how to love your brother or sister even when that brother or sister is in a really different place than you?

The weakness of ordinary family life gives all of us an opportunity to care for each other, to love each other even when it's difficult. This kind of opportunity can be a real gift from God, who uses these opportunities to show us how love works.

The grace of weakness frees us from trying to be something we are not. It frees us to love our parents or children or spouses even when we find out they're not superhuman. It frees us to take care of each other when we're tired or cranky or just plain annoyed. It frees us to accept the love of our ordinary, disappointing families instead of wishing for something that isn't real.

It's because of who Jesus is and what He has done that our own weakness can be used for God's power. Ordinary things matter to God. Weak things matter to God. Instead of longing for a kind of perfection we don't have, we can think about the ways God uses us in our weakness.

HOPE IN THE BIBLE

If God loves weak, ordinary people and families, what should we do with the idealized family represented by the Cullens?

Shouldn't we still try to move toward that ideal? To be people who don't fail one another? Who love each other through thick and thin?

Well, yes and no. God does, often, give us the strength to be better families than we would otherwise have been, but God doesn't do this by taking away our disappointing families and replacing them with some impossible ideal. God gives us strength *through* our ordinary lives, not instead of our ordinary lives.

More importantly, God frees us from having to put our hope in an impossible ideal of a family, an ideal that can never be achieved. Christians recognize that the things wrong with the world—with us as individuals and with our families—are big things. Bigger than we could ever fix on our own. From a position of weakness, we receive the good news that only Jesus Christ can fix all that is broken.

Because Christian hope is firmly in Jesus Christ and no one else, we have no need for perfect families to save us. Since our families are all flawed, human, and weak, this is very good news indeed.

The Right Place for Family

But wait, aren't Christians interested in family values? Don't we hope that our families are places where God's goodness and love are shared? Places where the world can see that goodness and love?

We do hope for God to transform our families, but we have to put our hope in the right place. Hope is in Jesus, not in our parents or children. We should be warned, then, against idealizing the family. Pictures of perfect families offer false hope. They can make us dissatisfied with our own families when those families are doing the best they can in the midst of weakness. They can lead us to try to force our family life into a kind of perfect mold and thus rob us of the freedom to experience God's grace through imperfection.

Author Amy Laura Hall talks about a "sense a woman carries with her that she, and her home and family, are surrounded by and being scrutinized by the images of perfect domesticity they find in the pages of popular magazines."[4] Have you felt the pressure to make your life or your family life conform to some image of perfection? It can be so crippling, so tyrannical, to live constantly with this sense of being scrutinized.

Hall suggests that we think about the ways messy, imperfect, normal families are actually much better witnesses to God's goodness and grace than perfect, airbrushed families could ever be. Messy, imperfect, normal families have the freedom to be honest and real with one another, to acknowledge mistakes and limits, and to love one another anyway. Perfect, airbrushed families aren't free to give that kind of love. They have to work all the time to measure up, to have spotless countertops and

---

4. Amy Laura Hall, *Conceiving Parenthood: American Protestantism and the Spirit of Reproduction* (Grand Rapids: Eerdmans, 2008), 391.

well-groomed children. What a witness to God's goodness and mercy it can be when we love each other *because* we are limited and broken and human.

I fear that the images of family in Twilight may encourage us to think that we have to be glittering, immortal Cullens in order to know happiness and love. I worry about how easily Bella leaves her imperfect family behind. In doing so, she isolates herself from the way they care for her. Even if their care is imperfect, they love her and want good things for her. Bella cuts herself off from the love and accountability they offer. By trading them in for the Cullens, she loses the opportunity and challenge involved in loving real, messy, imperfect human beings.

God's gift of family is a good gift. It's not perfect though. We can be grateful that we don't need a good and beautiful family to solve all our problems or to save us. Family will let us down. Christian hope, though, will not.

THINK ABOUT IT/TALK ABOUT IT

1. Do you have an image of the "perfect" family? Does your family try to put on a perfect face to the world?

2. Have you, like Bella, experienced the family as a disappointing place?

3. Are you tempted to "check out" of your family life when it disappoints and annoys?

4. Have you ever experienced God's grace through weakness? Through opportunities that ordinary life provides to care for and love other weak people?

5. How can ordinary, weak people reflect God's goodness to the world?

6. This chapter has argued that the family should not be idealized, that we should accept the weakness of our families, but this should *never* be understood as an excuse for abuse. If you or someone you know is affected by physical, sexual, or emotional abuse in your family, you need to get away from the abuse. Talk to someone—a pastor, a teacher, a friend—who can help. Visit www.stopfamilyviolence.org for resources for those experiencing family violence.

Chapter 6

→>—<←

For Eternity

*The Good, the Bad, and the Reality
of Marriage in Twilight*

BELLA'S FEELINGS ABOUT MARRIAGE are at odds with her wish to be with Edward forever. Why would a girl willing to become a vampire for her love balk at the prospect of marrying him? Though she is terrified of marriage, Bella eventually agrees to marry Edward and is ultimately happy in her choice. Her worries about marriage contrast with other views of marriage in the saga, in which marriage is shown as an ideal eternal commitment and the basis of a happy shared life for the couple. How do the different messages about marriage in Meyer's story help us to think about marriage from a Christian perspective?

MIXED FEELINGS

At the beginning of *Breaking Dawn,* Bella prepares to marry Edward. Once she is his wife, he will finally make her a vampire. Her agreement, though, has been given against her instincts. She panics at the thought of marriage and can't reconcile the idea with her wildly romantic feelings for Edward. She explains to him, "I'm not that girl, Edward. The one who gets married right out of high school like some small-town hick who got knocked up by her boyfriend!"[1] Bella associates marriage with reduced opportunities and disdains it as a traditional route that doesn't make sense for her. Her mother married young and has trained her to think of early marriage as a certain mistake, a mistake she's too smart to make. Despite Edward's enthusiasm and her own desire to be with him forever, she can't shake the negative feelings she has about marriage.

In contrast, Edward's feelings about marriage are all positive. He tells Bella about the kind of human being he was before he became a vampire so many years ago. Edward explains, "If I had found you, there isn't a doubt in my mind how I would have proceeded. I was that boy, who would have—as soon as I discovered that you were what I was looking for—

1. Stephenie Meyer, *Eclipse* (New York: Little, Brown and Company, 2007), 275.

gotten down on one knee and endeavored to secure your hand. I would have wanted you for eternity, even when the word didn't have quite the same connotations."[2] Edward is clearly not afraid of commitment, and he seeks marriage because he wants to be bound to Bella.

Neither of Bella's parents thinks the marriage is the best idea. She especially dreads telling her mother, whose past experience means that "early marriage was higher up on her blacklist than boiling live puppies."[3] Bella argues that people will assume the only reason two teenagers would possibly get married is if she were pregnant. Edward offers an alternative reason though. In his mind, two people their age would obviously marry because of love.

Edward offers to go to Vegas if Bella doesn't want to have a big white wedding. They end up, though, with an old-fashioned fairy tale wedding, one that pleases Alice and Edward as well as family and friends. On her wedding day, Bella is afraid to look in the mirror and see her image in her wedding dress. She's sure the sight will make her panic, yet everyone agrees she is a stunning bride. Her beauty on her wedding day is a preview of the vampire beauty that will be hers when Edward finally transforms her. Marriage is the condition and, in some ways, even the cause of her moving from ordinary to extraordinary,

2. *Eclipse*, 277.
3. Stephenie Meyer, *Breaking Dawn* (New York: Little, Brown and Company, 2008), 17.

dissatisfaction to happiness, awkward teenager to gorgeous goddess. High expectations to place on marriage!

Any concern that she might panic, along with all Bella's ambivalence, evaporates the moment she actually marries Edward. Bella says, "I saw just how silly I'd been for fearing this—as if it were an unwanted birthday gift or an embarrassing exhibition, like the prom. I looked into Edward's shining, triumphant eyes and knew that I was winning, too. Because nothing else mattered but that I could stay with him."[4]

Once the wedding is over, Bella never regrets agreeing to marry Edward.

DESPISING MARRIAGE

Bella's negative feelings about marriage may resonate with readers of the Twilight Saga. The world has changed a lot in the past couple generations, and young women now have options besides early marriage. Bella associates marriage with the limiting of opportunities, and she has to go through a major change of heart before she can see anything good in marrying Edward.

More and more people are delaying or rejecting marriage. In 2008, the average age for a first marriage was twenty-seven for men and twenty-five for women. In 1950, men married at

---

4. *Breaking Dawn*, 49.

an average age of twenty-three and women at age twenty.[5] In an article from the *Washington Post,* Mark Regnerus reports that "many women report feeling peer pressure to avoid giving serious thought to marriage until they're at least in their late 20s.... Actively considering marriage when you're 20 or 21 seems so sappy, so unsexy, so anachronistic. Those who do fear to admit it—it's that scandalous."[6] There are many reasons for this trend toward delaying marriage until later in life. Christians need to express concern about a number of those reasons.

One reason for delaying or even despising the idea of marriage is that we are afraid it will interfere with our personal freedom and our opportunities to complete our education and have successful careers. If we buy into this, we assume that the best kind of freedom is a freedom in which we are free *from* other people, from responsibilities and obligations that would keep us from being able to do whatever it is that we as individuals happen to like best. It also assumes that the best way to define *opportunity* is to think of it in terms of being able to make a lot of money, wield a lot of power, and demand a lot of prestige.

Christians, though, have exciting reasons for thinking

5. The U.S. Census Bureau makes these statistics available at http://www.census .gov/population/www/socdemo/hh-fam.html#history.
6. Mark Regnerus, "Say Yes. What Are You Waiting For?" *Washington Post* (April 26, 2009).

about *freedom* and *opportunity* in very different ways. Christian freedom is not the unrestrained ability to do whatever we want to do at any particular moment. This is a good thing, since that kind of freedom would leave us at the mercy of our worst tendencies and our most sinful inclinations. Jesus offers us a much more beautiful kind of freedom, not a freedom *from* any kind of guidance or responsibility but a freedom *for* loving and serving Him. Part of the good news of the Christian life is that "it is for freedom that Christ has set us free" (Galatians 5:1). Jesus gives us the ability to use this freedom to "serve one another in love" (verse 13). Without the power Jesus gives us, we're not free to serve and love. Instead, we're trapped by our me-first, self-absorbed wants. In giving us Christian freedom, Jesus enables us to care for others in everyday ways. He gives us the freedom, for instance, to serve people who are poor and suffering or the freedom to love and serve the people we have to live with day in and day out.

According to the good news that God offers us, opportunity may also look very different, in the Christian life, from the opportunity to be successful in the eyes of the world. Jesus gives us the opportunity to have truly good lives, truly abundant lives. He frees us from the power of sin and selfishness and shows us ways to live in love.

This means that worry about lost freedom or reduced opportunity isn't a Christian reason to avoid marriage. Marriage, in fact, may be a place where God can train us for this kind of freedom and offer us the kind of opportunity that will make us truly happy. It's by no means the only place where this kind of freedom and opportunity can happen, but marriage is one place where God can free us for lives that are not for us alone and give us the opportunity to know commitment and service to someone else. Yes, marriage comes with commitment and responsibility, but that is part of the joy of marriage.

I'm certainly not saying that all Christians must marry young or marry at all to know God's freedom and opportunity. I am saying that, as people who learn what freedom and opportunity are from Jesus and not from this world, we don't need to buy into Bella's fears or her tendency to despise marriage.

Bella also sees marriage as a far too ordinary response to her experience of wild love. We see a recurring theme in the Twilight Saga when Bella thinks through her feelings about marriage at the beginning of *Breaking Dawn*. That recurring theme involves a tendency to look down on ordinary, everyday human life. Bella sees her love as anything but ordinary, but she thinks of marriage as settling for the status quo:

> I briefly contemplated my issues with words like
> *fiancé, wedding, husband,* etc. I just couldn't put it
> together in my head.... I just couldn't reconcile a
> staid, respectable, dull concept like *husband* with my
> concept of *Edward.* It was like casting an archangel

as an accountant; I couldn't visualize him in any
commonplace role.[7]

Again, though, God loves the ordinary, common things of
this world. God uses them and works through them. A loving,
faithful marriage is not "staid, respectable, dull." It is a place
where God's goodness can be shown to the world and where
God can do new things in our lives. Marriage is a good gift
from God.

Romanticizing Marriage

We must reject the all-too-easy road of simply despising marriage. At the same time, we need to reject another problematic
option: glorifying and romanticizing marriage. Many of us resonate more with Alice's joy in putting together a dream wedding
than with Bella's hesitation about dresses, flowers, and public parties. Little girls are taught to dream about their wedding day.

We also live in a society in which "dream weddings" have
become big business. My parents, like most people their age,
had a wedding reception in their church basement. There were
sandwiches, cake, and punch, and my grandmother made my
mom's wedding dress. My husband and I got married at church
too, but we had a big party afterward with dinner and dancing.

---

7. *Breaking Dawn*, 6.

My mom and I bought my dress at a fancy boutique. When I look back on my wedding day, though, the joy I remember has almost nothing to do with the money we spent on a party and everything to do with commitment to my husband, being surrounded by the people we love, and celebrating marriage with a wedding service that was about worshiping God.

The industry that sells weddings to brides and grooms has grown enormously since I got married. There are a lot of social pressures, for brides especially, to keep up with the trends and try to have everything perfect. It's routine for people to go deep into debt to pay for their "dream wedding." There are jokes about "bridezilla," a bride who becomes so focused on things going her way that she becomes a horrible, selfish monster who gives no thought to people around her.

There's nothing wrong with celebrations, and there's nothing wrong with the excitement that surrounds them. It is easy, though, for a wedding to be about social pressure, big spending, and turning the bride into the star of her own show. It's easy for it to become a selfish production when it ought to be about a community celebration of two people's promise to be faithful to each other and to serve God side by side.

All of the expense and excitement of the fairy tale wedding can be a distraction from the goodness and difficulty of marriage itself. It can also contribute to putting marriage into a place where it does not belong in human life, to making marriage the dream that a young woman lives for. The most important thing Christians can do when thinking about marriage is to choose a partner wisely. When we turn marriage into a fairy tale dream, a dream that we have to pursue no matter what, we are in real danger of choosing poorly.

A Christian marriage is on solid ground when both husband and wife are centered on Christ and trust that being married to *this* person will help them to better love and serve God. Both people being Christians, though, is not all it takes. If we're to marry, we'd better marry someone kind, someone who supports and respects us, someone who will shoulder responsibility. Other people can help us to see if we are choosing wisely, but a fuzzy dream of a wedding day can make it hard to see the wisdom of our choices.

Centering all our dreams on marriage can make it difficult to see that happiness and fulfillment are found in God and not in another person. Happiness and fulfillment are certainly not found in being a princess for a day. We don't have to be married to be happy. We don't have to be married to be fulfilled. We don't have to be married to grow up. The suggestion, in the Twilight Saga, that Bella needs marriage to be fulfilled is a dangerous one.

ANOTHER POSSIBILITY

In our culture, we don't have much of a concept of the single life as a significant and important one. There is certainly no strong, positive portrait of the single life in the Twilight Saga. People may delay marriage, wishing to remain unattached, but singleness itself is not seen as a special way that God calls some people to live in relationship with Him. Christians have always affirmed that being single is a special way to love and serve God, not a negative thing we have to accept if we're not lucky enough to find our Edward. The Christian single life is a positive way of life with an important place in God's way of doing things.

In 1 Corinthians, Paul gives some advice to the folks in the church he's writing to about how we should think about marriage and singleness. The most important message that guides his advice is that "the time is short" (7:29). Paul, someone who was always looking forward to the return of Jesus, was deeply aware of the importance of time. He wanted all Christians, single and married, to devote ourselves completely to God, to use the very short time we are given to love and serve with all that we are.

Paul points out that singleness gives Christians special opportunities for devotion to God. As a concerned pastor, he tells the people in the church:

> I would like you to be free from concern. An unmarried man is concerned about the Lord's affairs—how he can please the Lord. But a married man is concerned about the affairs of this world—how he can please his wife—and his interests are divided. An unmarried woman or virgin is concerned about the

> Lord's affairs: Her aim is to be devoted to the Lord in
> both body and spirit. But a married woman is con-
> cerned about the affairs of this world—how she can
> please her husband. (1 Corinthians 7:32–34)

While Paul affirms marriage as a good thing, he doesn't
want anyone to forget that God is more important than anything. Being single creates freedom to devote life to God. With
love, Paul wishes for at least some in the church to have the
special freedom of the single life, a life that enables complete devotion to the Lord.

I think Paul would approve of the thoughts of writers
Christine Colón and Bonnie Field, who encourage Christians to reclaim the good of the single life and to celebrate the
ways that God is working there. They encourage us to "resist
the temptation to think that our lives will only really start
once we are married. Rather than existing in a holding pat-
tern, waiting for marriage, and basing our ideas of God's
faithfulness on whether or not he provides us with the spouse
and children we desire, we must work toward developing a
more complex faith."[8] These wise thoughts apply not only
specifically to the good of the single life, but generally to all
of us who are tempted to think that fulfillment or real life can

---

8. Christine A. Colón and Bonnie E. Field, *Singled Out: Why Celibacy
    Must Be Reinvented in Today's Church* (Grand Rapids: Brazos, 2009),
    224.

be found in any other place than in a relationship with the living God. We need to dream not of fairy tale weddings, but of the things that Jesus can and will do with our lives as He transforms us.

The Good of Marriage

Because most of the churches we know emphasize marriage so much, it might surprise you to learn that there have been times in history when Christians had to defend the idea that marriage is a gift from God. Some people even claimed that marriage is evil. In the ancient church, an African pastor named Augustine took on the task of defending marriage to people who believed sex was shameful and the single life was the *only* good Christian life. Augustine's thoughts about the good God works through marriage have influenced other Christians down through the centuries. He names three good things God does through Christian marriage: faithfulness between married couples, the good of children, and the way marriage can direct people toward God. Selfish human beings are capable of making marriage a very bad thing, but God uses these three good things to turn us away from our selfishness.

The first good of marriage comes in the faithfulness God creates between married couples. While we, as selfish people, might want marriage—and life—to be all about ourselves, married life requires that we're constantly concerned about our spouse and not just about me, me, me. I've already talked a little bit about how unusual faithfulness is in our world. Because faithfulness goes against the grain in our culture, it can be a sparkling witness to the goodness of God. It lets husbands and wives show each other God's goodness, and it lets married couples show God's goodness to the world.

Jesus tells us about the importance of faithfulness when He speaks out strongly against divorce. Jesus reminded people that faithfulness was part of God's good intention from the time of creation: "Haven't you read...at the beginning the Creator 'made them male and female,' and said, 'For this reason a man will leave his father and mother and be united to his wife, and the two will become one flesh'? So they are no longer two, but one. Therefore what God has joined together, let man not separate" (Matthew 19:4–6). Jesus explains that divorce had been allowed because of the hardness of human hearts but that God does not intend for things to be this way.

Faithfulness is more than staying married and not cheating on your wife or husband. The good of faithfulness is also found in the everyday relationships of marriage. It isn't easy to remain faithfully kind, day in and day out, year in and year out. It isn't easy to remain faithfully supportive. It isn't easy to keep faithfully doing part of the work of the household—taking out trash, paying bills, earning paychecks, washing dishes—work that has to be done for people to live together happily and peacefully. In every marriage, there will be slips in this kind of faithfulness, moments when spouses forget to be respectful and caring. Mutual service isn't easy. Over time, though, marriage can be a boot camp for learning day-to-day faithfulness, and this kind of faithfulness can be a wonderful witness to God's love.

The second good that comes of marriage is the good of having children. I'll talk more about children in the next chapter, but for now it's important to realize that the gift of kids is one of the very good gifts God gives in marriage. As selfish people, we might want life to be all about us, but being a parent requires that we love and care for our children.

In the gift of children, we see that marriage is not just about the two people who said "I do." Marriage is also supposed to be good for *other* people. Marriage ought to show God's love and goodness to children. This goodness of marriage can go beyond a couple parenting and loving children in their own home. God can use marriages to show love to other people, people outside of a family. Maybe a couple shares this kind of love in teaching a class, in serving people who need it, or in having a generous home where hospitality spills out to many people. At best, marriage lets a couple come together to show God's love to the world in ways they wouldn't have done alone.

The third good of marriage is found in the way it can direct people toward God. When Augustine talked about this gift in marriage, he said that the first two gifts—faithfulness and children—are good for all married people, but this third gift is a special blessing in Christian marriage. In the unity between married couples, we see a sign of the unity between people and God. Marriage is a good thing, but that doesn't mean that keeping a marriage going isn't a hard thing too. Christian couples will find that they have to turn to the power of God if they hope for marriage to be any kind of witness of love to each other, to their children, or to the world.

Marriage, through God's power, can be a beautiful witness to real love. Anyone who has been married for a while can tell you that real love doesn't always look like the frenzied romantic love we admire in stories and movies and that we admire between Bella and Edward. Real love is based on God's love. It trains us to be less selfish and to care more about other people—husbands or wives, children or strangers—and, even better, it trains us to rely on God and to rest in His perfect love for us.

⸸ THINK ABOUT IT/TALK ABOUT IT

1. What are your own feelings about marriage? Are they, like Bella's, mixed? Do you despise or romanticize marriage?

2. What are the dangers of looking down on marriage? Of focusing all our dreams on marriage?

3. Do you know any inspiring examples of Christians who are devoted to God in the single life? in marriage? How might their lives serve as models for you of how to witness to God's love?

4. Are there differences between a Christian under-
    standing of marriage and the understandings we
    run into in the world? How does God intend for
    marriage to be good?

Chapter 7

+>-<+

Monster Spawn or Precious Child?

Children in the Twilight Saga

MOST READERS OF THE TWILIGHT SAGA aren't surprised when the love story leads to a marriage, but Meyer throws her audience a curve ball when the newly married couple becomes parents. Pregnancies and children aren't usually featured in teenage love stories, and Meyer's loyal audience has had mixed reactions to this plot twist.

Bella gets pregnant on her honeymoon, and the baby, whom she loves, threatens to destroy her. The situation and her response to it raise a lot of questions for readers about our own feelings about parenthood and prompt us to think about God's gift of children.

The Baby Who Eats Her Alive

The logic of vampire existence as laid out in the Twilight Saga—the fact that vampires are technically dead and cannot physically change—suggests that it wouldn't be possible, but the newly married couple discovers that Bella is pregnant. Astonishingly and against all odds, Bella and Edward's marriage results in new life. The vampire and the human are going to be parents.

The first sign comes when Bella starts eating ravenously. Then, in an extremely short amount of time, she feels the baby move. Bella loves the child immediately and unconditionally. "From that first little touch," she says, "the whole world had shifted. Where before there was just one thing I could not live without, now there were two. There was no division—my love was not split between them now; it wasn't like that. It was more like my heart had grown, swollen up to twice its size in that moment. All that extra space, already filled. The increase was almost dizzying."[1] Her love for Edward connects easily with her love for her child.

Bella's gigantic hunger is an early indicator that this baby will make huge demands on her body. Edward instantly senses a threat to his love, and he reacts the same way he has reacted throughout the Saga. He's ready to do whatever it takes to rescue

---

1. Stephenie Meyer, *Breaking Dawn* (New York: Little, Brown and Company, 2008), 132.

and defend her. Furious and horrified at the realization that Bella is in danger, Edward is convinced the baby is unnatural, a monster. Bella completely disagrees. She's surprised, of course, and she never really wished or imagined she would be a mother, but when it happens, it seems completely natural.

Their honeymoon cut short by the unexpected pregnancy, which progresses much more quickly than the ordinary human rate of nine months, the couple hurries home.

It doesn't take long for the pregnancy's threat to Bella to materialize. Edward and Carlisle plan to end her pregnancy before it can do her harm, and Edward tells her, "We're going to get that thing out before it can hurt any part of you. Don't be scared. I won't let it hurt you."[2] Bella, though, is determined to protect her baby at any cost.

She finds an ally and defender in Rosalie. Rosalie and Bella have always rubbed each other the wrong way. They never understood each other, but now they are united in their determination to defend the baby. When she became a vampire, Rosalie lost the opportunity to be a mother, and this is one of her deepest regrets. In becoming pregnant, Bella has what Rosalie has always dreamed of, and Rosalie stands by her.

The situation is extremely serious. The half-vampire baby seems to be sucking the life out of Bella, nearly killing her as it grows. Bella's loved ones are only able to pull her through her

2. *Breaking Dawn*, 133.

pregnancy and give her the strength she needs to survive by providing her with human blood to drink. Even before she becomes a vampire, Bella turns to blood for her own survival and the survival of her child.

When Jacob finds out about Bella's condition, she is weak and dying. For once, he agrees with Edward about something and suggests that Edward force Bella to have an abortion. Jacob calls the baby "monster spawn."[3]

Eventually Jacob's werewolf pack finds out about the pregnancy, and they see it as a dangerous and unnatural threat, a threat they are obligated to eliminate. The werewolves decide to destroy Bella and her baby, and this causes Jacob to leave his pack and join the Cullens in defending Bella. He may be horrified by the pregnancy, but he'll still do anything to keep Bella safe.

Bella's vampire baby can only be born by causing its mother's death. Something about the vampire pregnancy has changed Bella's womb so that birth can't happen normally, which means her baby must be born by vampire C-section. Rosalie starts the operation, but she has to turn away from the human blood, and Edward literally chews the baby out of his wife with his strong vampire teeth. It's hard to imagine a more gruesome and grisly birth scene. There are broken bones and gushing blood. The birth is beyond dangerous for Bella. She

---

3. *Breaking Dawn*, 177.

gives every appearance of being dead. Edward and Jacob are certain they have lost her, but at the moment when the child's birth is killing her, Edward finally transforms Bella into a vampire by plunging a syringe full of his venom into her heart.

The baby girl is named Renesmee for Bella's mother, Renee, and Edward's mother, Esme. Bella celebrates getting through the difficulty and dangers of becoming Renesmee's mother: "I had done it. Against the odds, I had been strong enough to survive Renesmee, to hold on to her until she was strong enough to live without me."[4] After she's born, everyone in the family is completely devoted to the child and will do anything to guarantee her safety. Even Jacob, who had planned to kill the baby for hurting Bella, makes a complete turnaround. When he sees baby Renesmee, he imprints on her, finding his soul mate.

Just as the pregnancy progressed more quickly than is usual, Renesmee grows rapidly. Half vampires, apparently, have no long years of dependency to get through. Everyone who knows Renesmee loves her, and the whole family will do whatever they have to do to keep her safe.

LOVING LIFE

God is the creator of life, and as God's children, we give thanks for God's good gifts. This truth is the basis for a Christian

---

4. *Breaking Dawn*, 375.

attitude toward all life, an attitude in which we protect life and acknowledge God as the one who controls life, including the lives of those who haven't yet been born.

In the time of the ancient church, pagan Roman society was indifferent about the lives of the vulnerable. Ancient Romans would expose unwanted infants, leaving them outside to die, and abortion was common. Our society is also indifferent about the lives of the weak, and contemporary Christians, like our ancient brothers and sisters, must work to live in ways that express love and care for all life, for the lives of the vulnerable, and for the lives of the unborn.

Glen Stassen and David Gushee, teachers who've done a lot of thinking about ethics in the Christian life, challenge Christians to realize that loving life means loving life at all its stages. We're tempted to "choose death rather than life," not just at the beginning of life but also in the middle and at the end. Stassen and Gushee, though, hold out the hope that Jesus gives us "ways of deliverance" that show us how to "resist those forces that diminish and destroy life."[5]

Abortion often happens when mothers feel a sense of desperation. When women have no support—emotional, financial, or spiritual—they sometimes feel driven to abortion as the only way out of what seems like a hopeless situation. The church needs to find ways to offer real support to parents in

---

5. Glen H. Stassen and David P. Gushee, *Kingdom Ethics: Following Jesus in Contemporary Context* (Downer's Grove, IL: InterVarsity Press, 2003), 215.

these situations. Stassen and Gushee maintain that "the best way to be prolife is to deliver people from the causes of abortion."[6] Though Bella is determined to protect her pregnancy, her situation is also one full of desperation, and her one support is in Rosalie. Perhaps her story can challenge us to create situations in which pregnancy brings not desperation, but hope.

I am compelled by Bella's strong determination to protect the life of her unexpected little one. In our society, it is becoming more and more common for mothers to be advised to have abortions when the babies they are carrying are seen, like Bella's half-vampire/half-human daughter, as being "abnormal." Parents are offered genetic screening, and babies with Down syndrome and other genetic conditions are often aborted. It takes courage to go against social pressure and to love and protect vulnerable children as Bella did, and Scripture continually presses us to protect those who are most vulnerable and to defend those who have no defenders.

PREGNANCY, CHILDBIRTH, AND MOTHERHOOD

Bella is a brave mother, but other messages in her story are quite disturbing. The story plays up fears that pregnancy, childbirth, and motherhood are dangerous and that they might just destroy you. It's not uncommon to have some fear that motherhood

6. *Kingdom Ethics*, 227.

might ruin our bodies, rob us of our freedoms, and make us lose ourselves, but it's hard to imagine a more terrifying portrait of pregnancy and childbirth than the one we find in the Twilight Saga.

Pregnancy is not a disease, and childbirth is not a medical emergency. In a society where many people have never seen a baby being born, the gory vampiric C-section in *Breaking Dawn* may seem especially terrifying, but the birth of a baby can be an incredibly precious and happy event. It needn't be violent or dangerous.

Yes, babies change our lives, but no, they do not destroy us. Sure, pregnancy can be uncomfortable, but babies do not suck the very life from their mothers. Birth is certainly a dramatic experience, but it is not a kind of death. I don't want to idealize pregnancy and childbirth, but I do want girls and women, especially girls and women who haven't had babies, to know that there is so much that is good and precious about this part of female life. In the New Testament, being a mother is depicted as both a "calling and privilege,"[7] a gift from God.

There is some truth mixed in with the lie that motherhood destroys the mother though. Having a baby *is* a dramatic change in life. Pregnancy is not the cute and comfortable romantic thing that it looks like in the media's depictions of

---

7. Andreas Kostenberger, "Marriage and Family in the New Testament" in *Marriage and Family in the Biblical World,* ed. Ken M. Campbell (Downer's Grove, IL: Intervarsity Press, 2003), 272.

movie star moms. Among other things, pregnancy involves lots of trips to the bathroom, weird aversions to foods, nausea, and medical care that invades any sense of privacy you might have. Babies aren't just cute. They're also messy, drooly creatures who fill up lots of diapers. Unlike Renesmee, they don't grow up immediately. Babies need years of constant care, and it takes a long time before they're capable of saying "I love you" back to their moms and dads. Babies aren't cute accessories; they're living, breathing, needy human beings. Being a parent requires tremendous time and energy, and it isn't something to take lightly.

Yet despite the way children change us and the demands they make on us, this isn't a bad thing. The daily responsibilities of caring for children force us to love someone besides ourselves and to recognize our own selfishness. God can use parenting as a way to teach us to be less selfish, to train us to reflect God's love more closely.

Of all the events in the Twilight Saga, Bella becoming a mother has drawn the most disapproval from readers, and this has come from both fans and critics. Some have seen Meyer as glorifying teenage pregnancy. Others have regretted the way the story makes childbirth seem terrifying. For fans, though, I think feelings about this are more complicated. For those who've identified closely with Bella throughout her story, her sudden pregnancy and devotion to being a mother may be difficult to relate to. Motherhood just seems too foreign and too far away to many readers.

It can't hurt, though, for us to spend some time thinking about God's intentions for parents and children. Pregnancy should not be romanticized or glorified, but it also shouldn't be despised. In God's story, pregnancy makes sense as a good divine gift, a blessing that is part of marriage, something to be embraced and protected. We don't have to fear that pregnancy will mess up our bodies, because we know that bodies exist for the glory of God. I've never felt more pleased with my body than in seeing how it could nourish my babies. In God's story, the pregnant bride isn't devoured and destroyed by husband and child. Instead, husband and child can be seen as gracious gifts, as part of God's intention for a life meant for His glory.

LOVING CHILDREN

If thinking about Bella's unexpected baby gets us to think more about what it means as Bella does from the first, to love children, I hope that the *ways* we love children will be shaped by God's witness to us in Scripture. In looking for a biblical lens to help us focus our understanding of children, several big themes can help to shape our thinking and our actions. First, children are an important gift, a gift that comes from God. Second, God places parents and children in a relationship that He intends to be good for children and to teach them about God. Finally, Jesus treasures children and shows us that there is something about children that reflects His kingdom.

Again and again, the stories of Scripture present children as an important gift from God. This gift is part of God's good intentions for married couples, reflected in God's words at creation: "Be fruitful and increase in number" (Genesis 1:28). These words are words of blessing. The fact that children are a gift from God means that this gift isn't something that we human beings can control. This gift isn't ours by right. It belongs to God.

There are many stories in Scripture in which people who thought they would never have children suddenly and unexpectedly become parents. Abraham and Sarah were old, but God promised that they would found a nation and gave them a son, Isaac, even when it seemed impossible. Rachel was jealous of her sister Leah, who had many children, but God finally gave her a son. Elizabeth, the mother of John the Baptist, also becomes a mother against the odds and against her own expectation. Hannah prays for a child, and when her son Samuel is born, she dedicates his life to God.

In all these cases, we see that God is the author of life, the giver of children who surprise their parents and become the way that God keeps promises. It is God, not us, who grants life.

Because of this, giving birth to children and parenting children cannot be the most important thing in a person's life. God is always the most important. God tests Abraham by asking him to give up his son, Isaac, even though Isaac is the child

God had promised and the way God is going to use Abraham to do something important in the world.

Scripture also speaks to the ways that God intends a good relationship between parents and children to play out. Children are a blessing to their parents, and parents are supposed to care for their children. Parents have a responsibility to nourish the gift God has given. Scripture speaks of the importance of parents teaching their children about who God is and what God has done in this world.

This relationship between parents and children is supposed to be mutual. Both parents and children should reap good things from it. Children are to "obey your parents" (Colossians 3:20), and parents, in turn, are not supposed to "embitter your children, or they will become discouraged" (verse 21). When these words were written, no one would have been surprised to hear children being told to obey, but the charge for parents to be careful guardians of their responsibility was unusual. Parents have a responsibility to nourish and discipline, but they are supposed to do it in ways that reflect God's own love, not as tyrants.

In the Bible, we also see Jesus treat children in a special way, a way that His friends find surprising. In the book of Matthew, we read how Jesus "called a little child and had him stand among them. And he said: 'I tell you the truth, unless you change and become like little children, you will never enter the kingdom of heaven. Therefore, whoever humbles himself like this child is the greatest in the kingdom of heaven'" (18:2–4). Jesus's kingdom is a place where, like with children, status doesn't matter. Humility before God, obedience, and trust in the goodness of God are ways in which we all should be like children.

CHILDREN OF GOD

Whether we are young or old, children or parents, all human beings are children in relationship to God. All of us are vulnerable. All are dependent on God. All are loved and protected by our Creator, and all of us should come to God with the humility and trust that Jesus treasured in the little children He knew.

Some of us have wonderful parents and some have terrible parents, but no matter what our human parents are like, God is trustworthy and offers us unfailing love. In Jesus, God has given us everything that rightly belongs to His children. We aren't strangers; we're God's daughters and sons. We aren't beggars outside God's door, but beloved members of the family, children who God has made into "heirs" (Galatians 3:7, 29). God gives us the gift of a loving relationship with Him.

In 1 John, we read words of celebration and promise. We can delight in the facts that we are God's children and that God promises us good things:

How great is the love the Father has lavished on us, that we should be called children of God! And that is what we are! The reason the world does not know us is that it did not know him. Dear friends, now we are children of God, and what we will be has not yet been made known. But we know that when he appears, we shall be like him, for we shall see him as he is. (3:1–2)

✝ THINK ABOUT IT/TALK ABOUT IT

1. How did you react to Bella's surprise pregnancy in *Breaking Dawn*?

2. When you think about the possibility (or reality) of being a mother, do you tend toward romantic daydreams? terrifying fears?

3. Does reading Bella's story make you think differently about Christian attitudes toward life? about societal attitudes about abortion?

4. How should the portrait of children in Scripture influence your actions toward the children in your life?

5. Can you take comfort in the promise that you've been made a child of God? What does this mean in your life? What privileges belong to God's children?

Chapter 8

✦

Inhuman Strength

Twilight and the Good Life

EDWARD'S FAMILY IS UNITED BY a commitment to being "good" vampires. They strive against their dark natures. They make a tremendous effort to resist their thirst for human blood, and this effort is an intriguing part of the drama of the stories. The Twilight Saga implies that there are certain ways to think about what it means to be evil or to be good. It also has a specific understanding of the conflict between good and evil and how we can hope to live lives that matter.

Christians also have ways of thinking about goodness, violence, and the effort we make to be moral. These themes are central to our understandings of what is wrong with our lives and what God does to save us.

Vegetarian Vampires

While vampires thirst for human blood, Edward and his family choose to deal with their thirst by hunting large animals. Edward explains to Bella, "I'd compare it to living on tofu and soy milk; we call ourselves vegetarians, our little inside joke."[1] The blood of beasts and bears can keep them going, but it doesn't satisfy their most basic cravings or strengthen them in the same way human blood would.

The drama of the Cullens' choice to live without destroying human life comes from the understanding Meyer gives us of just how deeply they desire human blood. If the desire weren't so strong, so firmly rooted in who they are, their self-control wouldn't be so impressive. Moment to moment, day to day, they must be masters of their own dark urges.

Longing for human blood is basic to being a vampire. It's very much part of vampire nature, who vampires are at the depths of their being. Their physical characteristics are even designed to lure in their human prey. They're supernaturally strong, unbeatable hunters, and no human being stands a chance against them. On top of this, they're incredibly attractive, drawing people to them like bees are drawn to flowers. Edward rants against what he is when he tells Bella, "I'm the

---

1. Stephenie Meyer, *Twilight* (New York: Little, Brown and Company, 2005), 188.

world's best predator, aren't I? Everything about me invites you in—my voice, my face, even my smell. As if I need any of that!"[2]

As she gets to know Edward, Bella recognizes that murdering humans simply *is* vampire nature. She asks him, "Why do you do it? I still don't understand how you can work so hard to resist what you…are. Please don't misunderstand, of course I'm glad that you do. I just don't see why you would bother in the first place."[3] Most vampires don't bother. Many of the tensest moments in the stories come when vampires follow their natures by taking human life. Bella sees the Volturi bring in a large group of people to murder, and she shudders at the way they indulge their bloodthirsty natures without any hint of hesitation or remorse.

VIOLENCE

The goodness of the Cullens and the moral fabric of the universe Meyer has constructed are based on a rejection of violence. At the same time, violence remains an important part of the stories, and most of the characters engage in battle and in the killing of enemies.

Edward's brother Jasper has a particularly violent past. As a new vampire, he was used by a power-hungry vampire

2. *Twilight*, 263.
3. *Twilight*, 306.

to try to gain advantage in vampire wars. He was responsible for a massive amount of killing. In explaining his past, Jasper reflects on the effects that participation in violence has on the moral life and on human relationships. Jasper believes that the "years of slaughter and carnage" turned him into "a monster of the grisliest kind."[4] Living in violence ate away at who he was, damaging his basic character. He also believes that violence damages relationships with others, making it difficult to form lasting bonds. "When you live for the fight, for the blood," he says, "the relationships you form are tenuous and easily broken."[5] The Cullens' friend Eleazar, also a vegetarian vampire, confirms Jasper's insight about the way that living without violence fosters close relationships. Eleazar explains that "abstaining from human blood makes us more civilized—lets us form true bonds of love."[6]

Many aspects of the Twilight Saga, then, work as a critique of violence. The characters value human life and the ability to live in peace. They see that violence changes individuals and communities by destroying compassion, trust, and the ability to form close ties with others. The Cullens are

---

4. Stephenie Meyer, *Eclipse* (New York: Little, Brown and Company, 2007), 300.
5. *Eclipse,* 299.
6. Stephenie Meyer, *Breaking Dawn* (New York: Little, Brown and Company, 2008), 603.

willing to fight against their most basic impulses in order to live without violence.

But other aspects of the stories make violence appear in a more positive light. Violence is seen as a natural response to any threat, and the male characters are described as prone to fighting and revenge. All the books include threatened battle or fighting, though in *Breaking Dawn* the actual battle is avoided even though the characters have trained carefully for it.

In many ways, the vampires in the story are more aware of the moral difficulties of violence than Bella is. Though the werewolves and vampires in her life don't reject violence when they're threatened by enemies, they certainly don't take it lightly. At one point, Edward turns to Bella in disbelief and says, "I just beheaded and dismembered a sentient creature not twenty yards from you. That doesn't bother you?"[7] In fact, it doesn't bother Bella.

As Christians, we follow a Lord who is the Prince of Peace. He counseled His followers to reject violence, and He Himself submitted to death when many people would have preferred Him to lead a violent rebellion against the government. Christians don't all agree about how to live lives that are faithful to Jesus in this regard. Some believe that Christians can engage in violence in order to protect the weak. Others are convinced that

---

7. *Eclipse,* 558.

the most faithful witness to Jesus's love comes when we refuse all violence, even if it means that we, like Him, pay with our lives. While Christians don't agree about exactly how to respond to violence in this world, we do agree that violence should not be taken lightly. Perhaps the role of violence in the Twilight Saga can provide some food for thought as we think about the ways violence damages our world and the ways we can be witnesses against that violence, witnesses to God's love.

RESISTING WHAT THEY'VE BECOME

Carlisle's story explains why he and his family make the tremendous effort needed to reject who they are and fight against their own natures, against their very selves. We learn that in Carlisle's human life, he was the son of a fanatical preacher, a man who hunted darkness and evil in all forms and devoted himself to destroying vampires. Carlisle joined his father's hunt and suffered a vampire bite. When he realized he was becoming one of the monsters his father was so intent on destroying, he had a crisis. He couldn't reconcile himself to living as an evil being. In pain and self-loathing, he struggled against the urge to take human life that was now a part of who he had become.

He became determined that he would reject life as the murderous creature he'd once hunted, that he could overcome his new nature and longings and refuse to destroy human life.

Carlisle describes this as a choice he made, an act of will. "Like everything in life," Carlisle explains to Bella, "I just had to decide what to do with what I was given."[8] In this case, though, what he had been given was a nature that longed for human blood, and his decision to reject that nature was in no way an easy one.

Carlisle's basic moral character is shaped by his past as a human being who defended others against evil. His compassion for others marks both his human and vampire lives. He rejects his father's zealotry and closed-mindedness, but he holds on to at least some aspects of the faith of his upbringing. He tells Bella, "I didn't agree with my father's particular brand of faith. But never, in the nearly four hundred years now since I was born, have I ever seen anything to make me doubt whether God exists in some form or the other. Not even the reflection in the mirror."[9] Carlisle explains, "I'm sure all this sounds a little bizarre, coming from a vampire. But I'm hoping that there is still a point to this life, even for us. It's a long shot, I'll admit. By all accounts, we're damned regardless. But I hope, maybe foolishly, that we'll get some measure of credit for trying."[10]

Carlisle's faith and hope in God are vague though. He believes in God "in some form or the other," but he doesn't have

8. Stephenie Meyer, *New Moon* (New York: Little, Brown and Company, 2006), 35.
9. *New Moon,* 36.
10. *New Moon,* 36.

the specifics about God as revealed in Scripture that would give his hope some direction. He hopes for goodness and purpose in life, but he doesn't have a distinct place to put that hope.

HUMAN NATURE AND HUMAN EFFORT

In the world of the Twilight Saga, good stands up against evil, and people struggle heroically to combat their own worst desires. The universe Meyer has created is, without a doubt, a moral universe, but the rules of goodness in that universe have crucial differences from the way Christians understand goodness and morality to work. Let's think about the ways we try to be good and the kind of creatures we are, and I'll clarify the differences between the picture of goodness we get from the Twilight Saga and the good news about goodness that God offers to us.

The vampire desire for human blood is deep and strong, but it is also something that can be defeated. Though the Cullens crave blood, they are able, through effort and practice, to keep the impulse at bay. As Carlisle explains things, "Just because we've been…dealt a certain hand…it doesn't mean that we can't choose to rise above—to conquer the boundaries of a destiny that none of us wanted. To try to retain whatever essential humanity we can."[11] At first, this looks inspiring. It appears

11. *Twilight*, 307.

to be an image of moral courage we can all aim for, but there's a serious flaw in this way of thinking. That flaw reveals that this image of moral courage is not inspiring. It's actually a recipe for despair.

The flaw, the great untruth, in the moral world of the Twilight Saga is the belief that human beings *are able* to rise above the darkness of our natures. This untruth is dangerous because if we believe it, we will be trapped in a hopeless place where we're always trying to dig ourselves out of the deep holes we're trapped in when there is simply no way for us to rescue ourselves. We can't work up our courage and make ourselves be good. We can't overcome our own evil.

There's good news though — the best of news — behind this terrifying image. God can and does rescue us. God can change our sinful natures into something new and good. God offers us transformation — not transformation we *achieve* through our own desperate efforts, but transformation we *receive* as a gift.

In the Twilight Saga, human beings are free to choose good or evil. When Carlisle hopes for goodness, he's hoping to hold on to his essential humanity. Even when that human nature is distorted by a vampire's bite and the human becomes a monster, Carlisle discovers that enough goodness remains, enough ability to fight against evil lingers, that a vampire can reject the thirst for human blood. In the Saga, then, the moral life is a choice to be made. Goodness is an option for all, human or vampire, who will make the required effort. Choosing goodness isn't easy, but it's certainly possible.

The Cullens hope God will see their effort and reward them. Edward isn't at all optimistic about the question of whether he can still have a relationship with God, but Carlisle finds great comfort in Edward's goodness. He sees that goodness as evidence that God will look on Edward favorably. Carlisle tells Bella, "I look at my...son. His strength, his goodness, the brightness that shines out of him—and it only fuels that hope, that faith, more than ever. How could there not be more for one such as Edward?"[12] Bella agrees that the goodness the Cullens have worked to achieve must be something that God would reward. Her thinking about the implications that being a vampire might have on eternal relationships with God ends with her conclusion that "I couldn't imagine anyone, deity included, who wouldn't be impressed by Carlisle. Besides, the only kind of heaven I could appreciate would have to include Edward."[13]

The portrait of the good life we find in the Twilight Saga matches the understanding of human nature held in the Mormon faith. There are several crucial differences between this picture of the good life and the good news of Jesus Christ.

12. *New Moon*, 37.
13. *New Moon*, 37.

→>-<←-	In the Twilight Saga	In the Gospel Story
Human nature	flawed, but essentially good	good as created by God but broken by sin
Evil desire	runs deep and strong but can be overcome	key to who we are and what we want; we can't turn away from it
What is possible	free to choose good or evil	trapped by sin
Effort	vigorous effort can make you good; the harder you work, the better you'll be	nothing we can do will make us good
Escape from evil	comes through moral effort, which God will reward	comes through the grace of Jesus; a gift we do nothing to earn
The good life	requires constant striving	is a gift God gives us; God transforms us

Because we are sinful creatures, born into a sinful world, we are no longer free to choose good or evil. Sin has wrapped us in heavy chains, and we can't escape. Human beings are broken creatures, and we have no way to break free from our love of sin, and sin isn't just an individual choice. Sin infects the world and changes what it means to be human. I can no more *choose* to turn my back on sin than I can *choose* to grow six inches. I can no more *will* myself to live in goodness than I can *will* my hair to start growing in lavender and curly instead of brownish and straight. I can no more *decide* to climb out of the hole I am stuck in than I can *decide* to learn to fly.

In Romans, Paul explains that "righteousness from God comes through faith in Jesus Christ to all who believe. There is no difference, for all have sinned and fall short of the glory of God, and are justified freely by his grace through the redemption that came by Christ Jesus" (3:22–24). Righteousness— being good and right in God's eyes—doesn't come from our own moral efforts, even the most strenuous efforts. There are no exceptions from the rule of sin. All people are caught in sin. Being good and right in God's eyes is a gift He gives through faith in Jesus.

In recognizing that we can't make ourselves good by our own efforts, we can find true freedom. God can set us free us from all our desperate and hopeless attempts to make ourselves worthy. Are there things about yourself that you think will never be good enough? Things you keep hidden because you're convinced God couldn't love you if your weakness showed? Maybe you're someone who constantly sets goals and boundaries, resolving to do better, and then ends up yelling at yourself because you've failed once again. Maybe you don't bother to set goals because you're so beaten down and discouraged by your own repeated failures. If you're frustrated by your own efforts to be good, you're not alone. God can set us free from all of this, from all our self-loathing and useless efforts to make ourselves into the people we think we ought to be.

We cannot force ourselves to be good. Sinful human nature is drastically unlike vampire nature in the Twilight Saga because it *cannot* be overcome through effort or will. Human beings are trapped by sin. We are mired in our dark desires in ways that we cannot shake free. This may sound negative, gloomy, and hopeless, but it is truly incredibly good news. It sets us free from our useless efforts to save ourselves, to force ourselves to be good. Understanding the way we are trapped can help us understand just where our hope lies. We need the grace of Jesus Christ if we are to hope for transformation. We tremble in need of grace. We are broken and in need of healing.

GRACE, GRACE, GRACE

God pours grace over us. Tons of it. Amazing grace. Abundant grace. Overflowing grace. God gives us countless good gifts, and He doesn't give them because we're deserving. God doesn't give them to us because we put forth a lot of effort. God's gifts are given freely, graciously. There are no conditions we have to meet before we can be worthy to receive them. God gives grace to save us, grace to transform us, and grace to make us truly good. All of it comes to us even though we're broken, even though we've failed, even though we sin.

The book of Romans tells us about this free grace. "You see," Paul says, "at just the right time, when we were still powerless, Christ died for the ungodly. Very rarely will anyone die for a righteous man, though for a good man someone might possibly dare to die. But God demonstrates his own love for us in this: While we were still sinners, Christ died for us" (5:6–8). Notice how Paul points out that we didn't have any power in all this. God shows us His love by offering us something we can never make ourselves ready for or worthy of.

THE GOOD LIFE

We're set free from useless striving to make ourselves good. This doesn't mean, though, that God doesn't have good plans for us or that we can be content with sin and evil. In Romans 6, Paul connects God's gift of grace in making us right in His eyes to God's gift of grace in making us good and setting us free from the sin that entraps us. "What shall we say, then? Shall we go on sinning so that grace may increase? By no means! We died to sin; how can we live in it any longer" (verses 1–2)?

Later in the same section, Paul gives us a description of the good life God intends for us:

Count yourselves dead to sin but alive to God in
Christ Jesus. Therefore do not let sin reign in your
mortal body so that you obey its evil desires. Do not
offer the parts of your body to sin, as instruments of
wickedness, but rather offer yourselves to God, as
those who have been brought from death to life;
and offer the parts of your body to him as instruments of righteousness. For sin shall not be your
master, because you are not under law, but under
grace.

What then? Shall we sin because we are not
under law but under grace? By no means! Don't you
know that when you offer yourselves to someone to
obey him as slaves, you are slaves to the one whom
you obey—whether you are slaves to sin, which
leads to death, or to obedience, which leads to righteousness? But thanks be to God that, though you
used to be slaves to sin, you wholeheartedly obeyed
the form of teaching to which you were entrusted.
You have been set free from sin and have become
slaves to righteousness. (verses 11–18)

Oh yes, Christians believe in the good life, but that good
life isn't something we can win through our own efforts. Instead, we trust in God's goodness, goodness God shares with us
as a free gift. In that gift, God changes us, setting us free from

the chains of sin and opening up new possibilities for us. What would have been impossible through human effort is given to us through God's grace and goodness.

† Think About It/Talk About It

1. What's your reaction to the idea of vegetarian vampires? What does it say about what it means to be good?

2. Does the Twilight Saga help you rethink your attitude toward violence?

3. What are the key differences between the good life in the Twilight Saga and the good life God promises in Scripture?

4. In what ways is your life affected by constant effort and striving?

5. How does God set us free from sin?

Chapter 9

‣>‹‣

My True Place in This World

Bella's Search for Purpose

THE QUESTIONS ARE OLD ONES, and they are one key to how the Twilight Saga connects with us as readers. What is the meaning of life? What's our purpose? What does it mean to be human?

Bella's story is certainly about purpose, about what her life is for. She struggles with herself throughout the series because of her desire for something more in life. Finally, in becoming a vampire and being united with Edward and his family, she finds transformation, purpose, and meaning.

Most of us, like Bella, struggle with the meaning of our lives and our place in the world. We, too, want something more, something that matters. What can we learn from Bella's search for meaning? From her transformation at the end of the series?

TROUBLE BEING HUMAN

At Bella's first encounter with the Cullens, she is floored by their beauty, which she describes as inhuman. This inhuman beauty is the opposite of Bella's perception of herself—she is, in her own reckoning at least, absolutely ordinary. Many readers can identify with her sense of dissatisfaction. She is clumsy and graceless. She doesn't feel like she truly belongs anywhere, either at home or at school.

As her story unfolds, Bella longs more and more deeply to stop being her plain human self and to share in the "inhuman" beauty of the Cullens. Part of her frustration with Edward's long refusal to change her into a vampire is her horror at growing older. Getting older, for Bella, symbolizes all her ambivalence about and even distaste for her ordinary human life. She sees Edward sparkling in the sun, beautiful, glorious, and frozen in time. He is forever young. Bella can only compare herself to him in negative ways. She doesn't shine. If Edward doesn't change her, she will grow old. She will fade and die.

We identify with Bella because we too feel ambivalence, even distaste, about those aspects of our lives that so easily seem meaningless. Plenty of people relate to Bella's belief that she is nothing special and doesn't particularly belong anywhere. Like Bella, we have issues with being merely human.

Yet there is so much to love about ordinary human life. It is clear in Scripture that God has good intentions for human beings. God intends purpose and meaning for us. In Genesis 1:27, we learn that human beings are created in God's image. This is an enormous claim, a valuable claim, a claim that ought to give us a purpose.

It's no small thing to reflect God. Over the years, Christians have done a lot of thinking about what it means for humans to be created in God's image but haven't been able to agree exactly *what* it is about us that reflects God's image. Scripture points to a variety of possibilities. Maybe it's that we, like God, are spiritual beings who can do spiritual things like think, speak, and hope. Maybe it's that we, like God, are meant to live in relationships. God didn't create us to be alone but to love each other and to love Him. Maybe it's that we, like God, have a responsibility for the rest of creation. As God is the creator, perhaps we're to reflect His image by being caretakers of creation. Maybe being in the image of God reflects some combination of these things.

Whatever else it means, Christians agree that to be created in God's image means something unshakable about the importance and purpose of human life. We are supposed to reflect the amazing, loving, perfect God who made us. This means our lives are valuable and meaningful in ways we often don't consider.

WANTING SOMETHING MORE

Why then do we, like Bella, still long for purpose and meaning that our ordinary lives don't seem to deliver? Because something has gone wrong with human life.

We were created in God's image, which means great things for us, but humans chose sin and death instead. Sin and death changed the whole world, and they changed human life too. While our purpose was to be carriers of God's image, reflectors of His glory, God's image in us is now tarnished. That image was broken by sin.

Of course, we long for something more. We are no longer what God intended us to be.

In Romans 8:22–23, Paul beautifully expresses this sense of longing:

> We know that the whole creation has been groaning
> as in the pains of childbirth right up to the present
> time. Not only so, but we ourselves, who have the
> firstfruits of the Spirit, groan inwardly as we wait
> eagerly for our adoption as sons, the redemption of
> our bodies.

We're not alone in wanting more. Something isn't right, and all of creation is waiting, groaning, and longing. And, Paul says, we human beings are included.

Those who belong to Jesus Christ have the "firstfruits" of the something more we crave. The Holy Spirit starts a good change and a good work in our lives, but that change is not complete. We're still eager, still groaning, still waiting.

What are we waiting for? For God to adopt us, to make us children in His family, by transforming our bodies. There is enormous promise here. All of our dissatisfaction will end in hope.

TRANSFORMATION

In many ways, Bella's final transformation is my favorite part of the Twilight Saga. At the end of the series, all of her dissatisfaction comes to an end. She finds, finally, a transformed life full of meaning, purpose, and happiness. As we think about our own hope in God's transforming power, there is, for Christians, a lot to think about in Bella's story.

All of Bella's struggles with herself and her own humanity end when she is transformed into a vampire. Where she was awkward, she is now supremely graceful. Where she was, in her own mind at least, ordinary, she is now a stellar beauty. Where she was average, she now excels in every way.

Bella thought she would never be anything special. She thought her life could never be important, that whatever purpose or meaning her life might have could only be of the most insignificant kind. After her transformation, though, she comes fully into her own. The ugly duckling has turned into the swan. "It was like I had been born to be a vampire," Bella says. "The idea made me want to laugh but it also made me want to sing. I had found my true place in the world, the place I fit, the place I shined."[1]

Isn't this what we all want? For our lives to truly matter? To find the reason we were made? To really belong somewhere in a way that makes our purpose clear? Bella comes to this joyful place where the pieces fall together, and at last, everything makes sense.

Newborn vampire Bella astounds the Cullens with her impressive skills and unprecedented self-control. Everyone expects her to be a helpless captive to her thirst for human blood. She, too, expects to lose herself, to be driven out of her mind by her new vampire desires. Instead, she is great at being a vampire. She is more herself than ever before.

Shortly after her transformation, Edward takes Bella out for her first hunt. They catch the scent of human blood, and Edward is terrified for Bella, positive she won't be able to control her urge to hunt and murder a human being. He is taken

---

1. Stephenie Meyer, *Breaking Dawn* (New York: Little, Brown and Company, 2008), 523.

aback when Bella is able to stop herself from pursuing the scent. Her self-control is unprecedented in Edward's experiences with new vampires.

Not only is vampire Bella highly skilled and in command of herself, but she also marvels at the way her transformation has heightened her senses and increased her love. "My old mind hadn't been capable of holding this much love. My old heart had not been strong enough to bear it."[2] Her ability to love—Edward, her child, her family—is intensified in ways she hadn't believed possible. She loves better than she could before. She even sees more clearly the beauty of her loved ones. Her transformed vampire eyes show her loved ones in a new light.

While her dissatisfaction and weaknesses have come to an end and her abilities have been heightened and become something new, she is still Bella. Her transformation doesn't mean that she isn't herself any longer. She still hates surprises. She is still incredibly uncomfortable receiving gifts. In her new immortal and beautiful face, Bella can still find herself:

I stared at the beautiful woman with the terrifying
eyes, looking for pieces of me. There was something
there in the shape of her lips—if you looked past the
dizzying beauty, it was true that her upper lip was
slightly out of balance, a bit too full to match the

---

2. *Breaking Dawn*, 426.

lower. Finding this familiar little flaw made me feel
a tiny bit better.[3]

There is both discontinuity and continuity between human
Bella and vampire Bella. She is new, but she is also old. That
"flaw" in her lip is evidence that the amazing, transformed Bella
is still the Bella Edward loves, the same Bella who wanted this
new life.

HOPE FOR CHANGE

As human beings created in God's image but in whom that
image has been broken by sin, we have a great hope. We hope
not just that God's image will be renewed in us—though that
alone would be amazing—but that God will finish the good
work He intends for us by completing in us a marvelous transformation. Because we can rely on the good promises God
made to us, we don't hope in vain.

Bella's transformation helps us think about Christian hope
for transformation, but ultimately, our hope is for something
more, something even better than the happiness she finds in
her new life.

The pinnacle of Christian hope for transformation is found
in the promise of the resurrection of the body. God will not

---

3. *Breaking Dawn*, 405.

leave us stuck in the mire of sin and death. Instead, God promises us a great change. This change will allow our whole human lives—body, soul, and spirit—to make sense and to serve the beautiful purpose for which we were made. This resurrection will transform us into human beings who are fully able to glorify God. We will be set free from all those things that, right now, get in the way of our ability to glorify God. We'll be set free from weakness, from sin, from death, and from our own worst tendencies so that we can be truly free for that delightful purpose for which we were created—glorifying God.

Unfortunately, Christians sometimes lose sight of our hope for the resurrection of the body. The earliest Christians worked hard to clarify that their hope was *not only* that their souls might fly away to heaven someday. Those Christians insisted their hope was much more, much better than that, because Christian hope for transformation is grounded in what we see in Jesus.

After Jesus suffered the agony of the crucifixion, after He was laid in the grave, He didn't simply rot there while His soul went off to be with His Father. No, Jesus was resurrected. He rose into new life, a transformed life, and His resurrection gives all Christians a bright glimpse at what God promises to us.

The promise of Scripture clearly links Jesus's resurrection to the resurrection all Christians hope for one day. This resurrection promises the transformation of our whole lives—not just our souls, but our bodies too. Early Christians were very firm about this understanding because it was threatened by other kinds of hope, false hopes popular in the ancient cultures those Christians faced. Many people in those cultures didn't think that hope, meaning, and purpose could have anything to do with this life or this body as we know it. These people thought the body was something irredeemable and this life was hopeless. In the face of this kind of despair, Christians worked hard to remind each other that God's power is great enough to redeem all things. This body and this life are included in Christian hope and Christian purpose.

Paul talks about the resurrection of the body in his first letter to the church at Corinth, telling his readers that all of us can hope to share in Jesus's resurrection. Just as "in Adam all die, so in Christ all will be made alive" (1 Corinthians 15:22).

Paul uses an analogy to compare the body as we know it in the here and now with the resurrection body. The body now is like a seed, and the resurrection body is like the tree that grows from the seed. There is both continuity and discontinuity in this analogy. An acorn and an oak tree are materially, physically continuous with one another, but at the same time, the oak tree is so much more than the acorn was.

The body now and the resurrection body are both continuous with one another *and* discontinuous with, or different from, one another. This continuity and discontinuity is very good news indeed. Continuity is good news because it means that our future hope can't be disconnected from our present. When we believe that God has a good purpose for us, we don't suppose that purpose is *only* in the future, with nothing to do with the here and now. The good things God intends for you and me are *for you and me.* Our ordinary human lives are good lives. They're lives God loves, and they're lives God won't give up on.

Discontinuity is good news too, though. Our lives, bodies, and purposes now are messed up. We struggle. We're weak. We suffer disappointment. People we love die, and we will face death too. But God promises to redeem all that. God promises to make it different, to make it new.

In that same chapter from 1 Corinthians, Paul talks about the differences between the body now and the resurrection body. The body now, he says, is perishable. The body now suffers dishonor. The body now lives in weakness. But in the resurrection, God will make all that new. The promised resurrection body will be, according to Paul, imperishable. Dishonor will be replaced by glory. Weakness will give way to power.

God promises a final transformation that takes all that we are, all that God has made us to be, and redeems it. Bella's transformation, in a way, mirrors our own hope. As it is Bella, and not someone else, who emerges on the other side of the transformation, so God promises to redeem us—*these* bodies, *these* selves. As Bella's past struggles are put behind her, God promises to free us from our weakness and suffering and disappointment.

Yet if Christians want to think about our hope and purpose, Bella's transformation won't be enough food for thought.

One of the most important parts of Paul's talk about resurrection clearly connects our hope for transformation to Jesus Christ. "Just as we have borne the likeness of the earthly man," Paul says, "so shall we bear the likeness of the man from heaven" (1 Corinthians 15:49). Christian hope for transformation is a physical, material hope. It is a hope that God's ultimate purposes for us will be continuous with who we are now and what God is doing with us now. It is also a hope for transformation beyond the problems and sufferings and weaknesses of the present. The verse I've just quoted, though, gives us the most important information we need about that hope. It is a Jesus-centered hope, a hope that we will "bear the likeness of the man from heaven."

Our meaning and purpose is not random. It is not about our personal preferences. It is not a choose-your-own-adventure brand of pie in the sky. In becoming like Jesus, the image of God is renewed in us. In reflecting who Jesus is and becoming mirrors of His love, we're able to again reflect God's glory. The purpose and meaning that were stolen from us by sin are offered back again in Jesus.

Our meaning and purpose are found in Jesus. As God transforms us and gives us purpose, we're going to find that transformation and purpose are all about Christlikeness. This is true of both our purpose now and our final, eternal purpose. It is about being transformed into the likeness of Jesus, God's own Son, someone who loved us and the whole world enough to enter into our situation and die for us. Jesus, in His resurrection, conquered death and promises us victory over death.

Even Meyer's immortal vampires aren't truly free from death. Granted, killing a vampire is more work than killing a human being, but the Volturi or some other enemy could still destroy them. Christian hope as we see it in Jesus, though, offers us a final freedom from this threat. No enemy can destroy what God promises. Death will finally be conquered; its terrible effects will be undone.

This hope is not just for the future. While the promise of bodily resurrection is the *final* hope of Christians, that hope changes our lives in the here and now. It gives us meaning and purpose, not just later but now. When we look at our lives right now, our bodies right now, we can see the beginning of the transformation God is working on. We can reject our tendency to despair about finding meaning because we know that our meaning is found in Christ.

Hope in God is a trustworthy hope. When we put all our hope in other things—in romantic love, a fairy tale marriage, or even our own interests—that hope is sure to disappoint. Because our hope in God is trustworthy, it's not just a future hope. It's very real in the present. Because we're people who live in hope, the resurrection changes our lives right here and now.

N. T. Wright puts it like this: "Because the resurrection has happened as an event within our own world, its implications and effects are to be felt within our own world, here and now."[4] Our lives and work in this world matter. If we're artists, our art matters. If we're poets, our poems matter. If we're athletes or bakers or gardeners, our sports and bread and flowers matter. Our relationships with God and other people matter too. Those relationships aren't just temporary things. They have a future. If we can show love, justice, or beauty to someone else in the here and now, that witness may have eternal implications.

Remember, Christian hope for transformation is a hope for continuity. I'm not longing to stop being myself. I'm longing for God to do something good with me. I'm longing for God to make me a reflection of His good purposes, and God starts this work in my life right now. As transformed Bella is still Bella, when God has finished transforming you and me, we will still be ourselves. Your body and soul and life right now matter. Because they belong to God, they have meaning and purpose.

☦ THINK ABOUT IT/TALK ABOUT IT

1. Do you identify with Bella's dissatisfaction with her ordinary life? With the slogan "Bella: Hope for clumsy girls everywhere"?

---

4. N. T. Wright, *Surprised by Hope: Rethinking Heaven, the Resurrection, and the Mission of the Church* (New York: HarperOne, 2008), 191.

2. Spend a few minutes thinking about the truth that human beings are created in the image of God. List some ways this should change the way we think about our own lives and the lives of all humans.

3. Where have you witnessed God's transforming power? God's power to bring light out of darkness? goodness out of sin? life out of death?

4. What are the features of Bella's transformation? Which ones might help us think better about Christian hope?

5. How does the Christian promise of transformation—the promise of the resurrection of the body—change the way you think about your life? your body? your purpose?

6. What would it look like, in day-to-day life, to "bear the likeness" of Jesus? What specific things about His life could be reflected in your own life?

Chapter 10

-+><+-

Passion for God

The Power of Desire in Twilight and in Real Life

DESIRE TAKES A CENTRAL ROLE in the Twilight Saga. There is deep desire for blood. There's Bella's desire for Edward and his for her. Bella's and Jacob's conflicted desire for each other. Edward's desire to marry Bella and Bella's to become a vampire. Sexual desire is worked through the entire series. There are desires for family, for closeness, for love. Desire to protect baby Renesmee and other loved ones. Desire to be strong, to be good, to be immortal. Perhaps most powerful of all, the desire to be transformed.

Desire is strong stuff. What we want shapes who we are. It shapes our lives, our actions, our time, and our commitments. Because of desire we go down one road and reject another. We're deeply shaped by our desires.

We are what we crave, and Christians have a compelling story to tell about how desire can be shaped by God.

LOOKING FOR LOVE (IN ALL THE WRONG PLACES)

Throughout this book, I've expressed concerns that the Twilight Saga encourages us to spend our desire on things other than God. Bella is constantly looking for fulfillment in all kinds of things. She focuses her hope on love with Edward, expecting to find happiness in an immortal vampire life shared with him. She's a clear example of what it might look like to suppose that your life can be made complete by someone else. She calls Edward the "core" of her existence.[1] Her desire for him is overwhelming, and she fully expects him to meet her needs and make her happy.

In various chapters of this book, I've suggested that it's a warning sign when we start pouring all our desire into one place or one person. When we put someone on a pedestal, that person is bound to come tumbling down. For instance, some of us center our hopes on families, wanting parents or children to be perfect, to be more than they can or should be. When our hope is centered on another human being, we're asking that person for something he or she can't and shouldn't give.

---

1. Stephenie Meyer, *New Moon* (New York: Little, Brown and Company, 2006), 312.

Dreams about love, romance, marriage, and even sex can take over our lives. Those dreams can control all our passions. We look to all kinds of things to transform us—exercise, food, education, love—but we're inevitably disappointed when these things don't deliver fulfillment.

At many points, Scripture describes the problem with human beings as a problem of desire. We want what we shouldn't want, crave what can never fulfill us, and throw our energy into loving things that lead us away from God. Second Peter 2:10 speaks of the "corrupt desire of the sinful nature."

Our whole beings are shaped by what we desire and love. Martin Luther taught "that to which your heart clings and entrusts itself is, I say, really your God."[2] Luther wrote this when teaching about God's command to "have no other gods" (Exodus 20:3). He recognized that whenever our hearts cling to things besides God, we are making false gods out of those things. Luther saw that we're likely to cling to and desire all kinds of things—money, learning, power, tradition, and other people. He begged Christians to see that the only place to put our trust and hope, the only thing worth clinging to, is God. Luther explains that it is as if God were speaking directly to us and saying, "Whatever good thing you lack, look to me for it and seek it from me, and whenever you suffer

---

2. Martin Luther, *The Large Catechism,* trans. Robert H. Fischer (Philadelphia: Fortress Press, 1959), 9.

misfortune and distress, come and cling to me. I am the one who will satisfy you and help you out of every need. Only let your heart cling to no one else."[3]

In Romans 8, the Christian life is described as a life in which desire is changed from the desires of sin to desires for the things of God: "Those who live according to the sinful nature have their minds set on what that nature desires; but those who live in accordance with the Spirit have their minds set on what the Spirit desires" (verse 5). The sinful nature is all about wanting the wrong things. It's about desiring things that aren't God and about getting deluded into thinking that those things will make us happy. We can't force ourselves to desire God instead of other things, but the Spirit helps us to see things as they are, to save us from loving the wrong things the wrong way, and to change our desires. When this happens, God begins to transform our whole lives.

WHAT WE WANT

In chapter 6, I talked about an ancient pastor named Augustine and his views on marriage as a good gift from God. Augustine was a good reader of Scripture and a good observer of the Christian life, and his take on being human has exercised

---

3. *The Large Catechism*, 9.

more influence over Christian thought than any other thinker down through the centuries—outside of Jesus and the biblical authors. Augustine believed desire was central to what it means to be human. He thought it was central to both what's wrong with us *and* to the way that God takes what's wrong and makes it right. His thoughts on the subject help us think about the ways our lives are controlled by the things we want and love.

As Augustine describes the situation, there are two ways to love something. We can love with a love of use, or we can love with a love of enjoyment. The love of enjoyment belongs only to the things that make us truly happy. That love of enjoyment—I suppose we could call it "true love"—happens when we love something for its own sake. The love of enjoyment means that we're satisfied with the thing we love; we're content with it as itself.

The love of use is a love that helps us get to that place of real happiness. The thing we love with a love of use is meant for a certain purpose—a use—and we love it because it does what it's meant to do. I might love my station wagon with a love of use. It's not particularly lovable in itself. Not many people get excited about a boring car like a station wagon for its own sake, but I love it because it does what it's made to do by getting me from point A to point B.

Augustine had a giant revelation in his life. He spent lots of time spending his desire on things that weren't God. He desired women, knowledge, and power. After a long and painful process, he realized that it's only God who makes us truly happy, and so he wanted to drive home the point that *only God* should be loved with that love of enjoyment. The only thing that is worthy of being loved for its own sake is God. Everything else will disappoint. Only God is truly lovable, which means we should love Him with true love, the love of enjoyment. Everything else—and Augustine really means it when he says *everything*—should be loved with a love of use.

Am I saying that we should love everything that isn't God—all the big loves that drive the Twilight Saga, like romance and family, children and marriage—with the love Augustine calls a love of use? We're supposed to *use* our loved ones? Augustine thinks we are. Before you close the book in disgust, hear him out.

Augustine thinks we should love *everything* that isn't God with a love of use because only God is lovable in His own right. More importantly, we're supposed to love everything that isn't God with a love of use, but we can only do that properly when we understand what exactly it is that everything is useful *for*.

In Augustine's way of thinking, everything has only one right use, only one proper purpose, and that is to love God.

He believes we're supposed to love everything, absolutely everything, that isn't God with the purpose of directing all of life toward loving and glorifying God. Love for God should be like a rushing river; the water should pour in one mighty channel in God's direction, and every other side stream or tributary ought to be collected into that one main river. Every drop of water, every bit of desire, the purpose of every love, ought to flow toward God.

When Augustine suggests that I should love God with a love of enjoyment and, say, my husband with a love of use, he isn't saying I should use my husband in the way we usually think of when we say, "She's using him." I'm not supposed to use him to take out the trash or earn a paycheck. I'm not supposed to use him to build up my self-confidence or help me feel less alone. I'm supposed to "use" him for the one purpose he's actually intended for. When God created my husband—and everything else—there was one reason. My husband is intended to exist for the love of God. So if I'm to love him with a love of use, my love for him should be *for God's sake.* My love shouldn't stop with him, as though he were the point of my life. Our love should point each other toward the purpose we're both created for, loving and glorifying God, who *is* love. Our love, instead of stopping with us, should flow through us and on to God.

You probably won't be surprised to hear Augustine's diagnosis of our human situation. We get loving wrong. We love the wrong things for the wrong reasons. Only God will make us truly happy. Only God is truly lovable, but we love everything else as though it could fulfill us. We love husbands and wives, children and parents, jobs and hobbies, and even pizza and cars as though they could make us truly happy. We love all these things for their own sakes. Then, to make matters worse, we love God, who truly *is* love, with a love of use. We love God because we think it might get us something—maybe loving God will get things to go our way. Or maybe we love God because we want a ticket to heaven. We love God to use Him and love everything else as though it will give meaning and purpose to our lives.

In Augustine's diagnosis, we human beings are victims of a major love disorder. He compares us to "wanderers in a strange country" who will only be happy when we reach our true home. As wanderers, we need to use things in order to make that journey home. We need some way to get there—a boat, a car, a train, a pair of running shoes—if we ever hope to reach that place where real happiness lies. The problem is that we get sucked into the country we're driving through, we get "engrossed" in false "delight," and instead of hurrying home, we hang out in a country that can't possibly make us happy.[4] We've gotten our loving, our desire, and our wanting all messed up. As sinners, we love everything but God as though it could fulfill us.

God can change our love, though. God can restore our desire so that we want what will make us truly happy, the thing we were intended for all along, a relationship with Him. It's

---

4. Augustine, from *Nicene and Post-Nicene Fathers,* First Series, Vol. 2, "City of God, Christian Doctrine," ed. Philip Schaff (Buffalo, NY: Christian Literature Publishing Co., 1887), "On Christian Doctrine," book 1, chapter 4.

God we're meant to truly enjoy. Only God is eternal and trustworthy.

PASSION FOR GOD

Desire is good thing. It's meant to be directed to and for God.

In Psalms, we get a strong picture of what it looks like to desire God. "As the deer pants for streams of water, so my soul pants for you, O God" (42:1). This is a great image, isn't it? Picture the deer, incredibly thirsty from running through the woods, literally panting to get to that drink. We humans are that deer, longing for and panting for God. The psalm continues, "My soul thirsts for God, for the living God. When can I go and meet with God?" (verse 2).

In another psalm, the author cries out, "Whom have I in heaven but you? And earth has nothing I desire besides you" (73:25). In Psalm 145, we read a song of praise to God for fulfilling what we want and need. "You open your hand and satisfy the desires of every living thing" (verse 16). Fulfillment is found in God. God satisfies our true desires.

God isn't in the business of getting rid of our passion or dampening our desire. God is in the business of *transforming* our passion and desire so that, instead of longing for all kinds of stuff that disappoints, we can pour our love out on the one thing that will truly satisfy.

Don't hear judgment in all this talk about desire. Don't hear me saying, "Shame on you. You have a love disorder. Shape up." Instead, hear a message of hope. We can't force ourselves to love God. We can't transform our own passions, but we *can* trust in God's overwhelming goodness to us. We can trust that the Holy Spirit can change what we crave. We can look at the promise that God will satisfy our desire, and we can find hope.

That boy or girl you want so much? You don't need him or her to complete you. God will satisfy. That man or woman who seems like he or she would finally make your life happy? True happiness lies only in God. That perfect marriage or family or parent or child you wish you had? You can let that image of taunting perfection go, knowing that only God can fulfill. The new life and transformation you long for? It won't come from self-help or from another person. But it can come from Jesus Christ. We can let go of our glittering Edwards and our other glittering idols and find freedom in Christ to passionately love this life as it's meant to be loved—for the glory and love of God.

The prophet Isaiah talks about the way God fulfills our desires, promising that "the LORD will guide you always; he will satisfy your needs in a sun-scorched land and will strengthen your frame. You will be like a well-watered garden, like a spring whose waters never fail" (58:11). Picture that eternal spring, the flowing fountain that will never run dry.

In God's love story, we find the only love that won't disappoint, the river that won't dry up, and the place where our passion will be returned.

All Bella Swan thought she desired to make her happy was Edward.

All we need is God.

✝ THINK ABOUT IT/TALK ABOUT IT

1. What kind of desires make the Twilight Saga tick? What role does desire play in other stories you love?

2. Describe Augustine's idea that there are two kinds of love. Does his explanation give you insight into your own life?

3. Where do you see people who are passionate about God? How can you learn from those examples?

4. What would your life look like if your love story were *first* about loving God? What unexpected things might God do?

Epilogue

–➤–◄–

Jesus, the Light

THE TWILIGHT SAGA STIRS UP the hopes of its many readers.

As I've led you through the themes of the saga, I've tried to point out that those hopes and desires aren't bad things. It's not wrong to dream of love (or marriage or family or transformation or any of the other dreams and hopes that are part of the saga). But if our hopes are raised by things bound to disappoint—as anything that isn't God is bound to disappoint in some way—I worry that we'll turn into sad cynics, people who look back on the dreams for love we once had and laugh at how false our hope turned out to be.

God can transform our hopes and desires, though, giving us a love story that will not disappoint. If this book has helped you begin to see some of those hopes differently or to ask questions about putting all hope in things that aren't God, then I'm glad.

My own hope, as you finish this book, is that you might catch a vision of the great hope that lies in God. God gives us a vision of hope in which we live in the bright light of Jesus's love.

The titles of Meyer's novels are all about light. Twilight is the time between darkness and light, the end of the day when the light is fading. The new moon provides just a sliver of light in the darkness. An eclipse blocks the light, keeping it from reaching us, but the breaking of dawn implies the coming of hope and the possibility of vision. Darkness threatens, but light breaks through. Stories of light and darkness capture our imaginations. They reflect our own stories, stories in which we struggle, in which we're in danger of being unable to see when we long to see clearly.

We live in a world of light and darkness, a world where we sometimes find ourselves stumbling through the shadows, unable to see the way ahead. Scripture is full of promises about the ways that Jesus brings us light. Everything was created through Him. Life is found in Him, and "that life was the light of men. The light shines in the darkness…" (John 1:4–5). Scripture promises that darkness has *not* overcome that light. People can be witnesses to the light, but none of us are ourselves that light. Jesus is "the true light" and gives light to all people (verse 9).

The vision of hope in the book of Revelation is a vision in which darkness has been driven away and we can see clearly in the light of Christ. God's "city does not need the sun or the moon to shine on it, for the glory of God gives it light, and the Lamb is its lamp. The nations will walk by its light, and the kings of the earth will bring their splendor into it. On no day will its gates ever be shut, for there will be no night there" (Revelation 21:23–25). We have a great hope, and we can trust in God's great promises. Darkness and evil will be overcome. God will destroy grief and death and sin and give us new life in the light of Jesus's perfect love. We don't have to look for anyone but Jesus to light the way for us.

Book-by-Book Discussion Guide

This guide is meant to encourage you to discuss the material in this book in relation to the four books in the Twilight Saga.

The questions in this guide are meant to get you thinking and talking about the events and characters in the books and your own reactions to them. These questions are more plot focused and less focused on the themes of the Saga or relating those themes to the spiritual life.

For each particular novel in the Twilight Saga, I'll suggest chapters in this book that would be helpful to discuss while discussing that novel. As you think about the themes of the Saga and the meaning of those themes for your life of faith, I encourage you to turn back to the questions at the end of each chapter in this books, questions that encourage you to think biblically about those themes.

Twilight

1. Why did you pick up the book? Did someone recommend it? Did you read it quickly?

2. Talk about the feelings reading the novel stirred up for you. Excitement? Annoyance? Longing? Cynicism? What events in the story contributed to those feelings?

3. When we first meet Bella, she is leaving her mom and home in Phoenix, embarking on a new phase in

her life. What do you think of Bella's independence? Does it represent something we long for as we grow up? Is it something more frightening?

4. Spend some time talking about Edward. Describe his character. What draws Bella to him? What frightens her about him?

5. Imagine you are in Edward's shoes when he first meets Bella. What factors contribute to the look of hatred he gives her?

6. Why does James fixate on Bella as his prey? What emotions does this raise for Bella and the Cullen family?

7. Think about *Twilight* in relationship to chapter one, "Forbidden Fruit: The Allure of Dangerous Romance." How is romance portrayed as a) dangerous, b) consuming, and c) fated?

8. What makes Bella and Edward soul mates? Are you more likely to question to the idea of the soul mate after reading this book?

9. In relationship to chapter two, "Dazzled: How Love Works in the Twilight Saga," how does Bella act as a satellite to Edward? What aspects of their love should raise questions for us?

New Moon

1. How does Edward's response to Jasper's attempt to

attack Bella change their relationship? Should Edward have responded differently?

2. Why does Edward's departure come so close to destroying Bella? What things, specifically, change for her when he leaves?

3. What role does Bella's friendship with Jacob play in her response to Edward leaving? What do you think of the way she deals with that friendship?

4. When they think they've lost each other, both Edward and Bella court death. What does this reveal about their relationship with each other? Their relationships with friends and family?

5. What do you think of the idea that the werewolves in the series exist for the purpose of fighting vampires? What makes the two groups natural enemies?

6. How does Victoria's pursuit of Bella contribute to the plot?

7. Discuss the role of the Volturi in the story. Why are the protectors of vampire society so feared and dangerous? What is implied by their old relationship with Carlisle?

8. What do you think of the reunion between Bella and Edward? How do they deal with the hurts that have passed between them? How will it change their future relationship?

9. In relation to chapter four, "The Superhero and the Girl Next Door: Gender Roles in Twilight," what gender stereotypes are at work when Edward leaves Bella to protect her? When she falls into depression without him?

10. In relation to chapter five, "Baseball and Loyalty: Twilight and the Ideal Family," how does Bella's loss of the Cullen family contribute to her despair at losing Edward?

Eclipse

1. *Eclipse* provides many background stories about the vampire world that we, as readers, didn't know before. How do the stories of the characters' pasts, the vampire wars, and the nature of newborn vampires contribute to the themes of the Saga?

2. Why does Victoria raise a vampire army to threaten the Cullens? What does their response to the situation reveal about the family?

3. Tension about whether Bella will become a vampire grows in this novel. What were your reactions to this tension? Did you want Edward to give in and change her? Were you hoping for a surprise?

4. What does Bella's love for both Edward and Jacob say about the nature of love? What do you think of the way she deals with the situation?

5. Why does Bella choose Edward over Jacob? What do you make of her choice?

6. How does the alliance between the vampires and the werewolves contribute to the plot and themes of the novel?

7. In relation to chapter three, "Body and Blood: Twilight's Take on Abstinence and Sex," what happens in the book to increase the sexual tension between Bella and Edward? How did you respond to their choice to wait to have sex until they are married?

8. In relation to chapter eight, "Inhuman Strength: Twilight and the Good Life," what events in the book portray the vampire effort to be good?

Breaking Dawn

1. How did you feel when reading about Bella's wedding?

2. Why do Edward and Bella have such different reactions to her pregnancy?

3. Describe the effects pregnancy has on Bella physically, emotionally, and spiritually.

4. When she is transformed into a vampire, why does Bella hide the excruciating pain? Do you think she did the right thing?

5. What is so surprising about vampire Bella?

6. What do the special gifts of the vampire characters,

especially Bella's shield and Renesmee's way of communication, say about the characters? About what is of value in their world?

7. What is the importance of the Cullens' gathering vampire friends from around the world in preparation for their stand against the Volturi? What light do these various vampires shed on vampire society? On the Cullen family?

8. Can you explain the Volturi response to the Cullens?

9. In relation to chapter six, "For Eternity: The Good, the Bad, and the Reality of Marriage in Twilight," do you think the story in *Breaking Dawn* tends to despise marriage or to romanticize it?

10. In relation to chapter seven, "Monster Spawn or Precious Child? Children in the Twilight Saga," how does Bella becoming a mother impact your own thinking about parenting and children?

11. In relation to chapter nine, "My True Place in This World: Bella's Search for Purpose," why is vampire life the right life for Bella? How does it help you think about your place in this world?

12. How could the series have ended differently? Are there characters you'd like to hear more from? How does the ending Meyer chose reflect the themes of her Saga?